Hope Stories
FOR THE HEARTLAND

Kerry Hoffschneider

Prairie Muse Books Inc
Lincoln, Nebraska
2024

©2024 by Kerry Hoffschneider
All rights reserved.
This is a true account.
Names, characters, places, and incidents
are the product of the author's experience.
Any resemblance to other persons is entirely coincidental.

No part of this book may be used in another work, with the
exception of critical reviews, may not be copied in whole or in part,
or stored physically or electronically without having been
purchased from the author or having gained
permission from the author.

HOPE STORIES FOR THE HEARTLAND
Paperback

Lincoln, Nebraska

Table of Contents

Foreword 5
To My Future Generations 7
Hell's Half Acre 13
The Guiding Star on Our Old Shed 17
"To realize one's destiny is a person's only obligation." 19
York County Fair 23
The John Deere 630 27
These Country Roads 31
Just up the road 35
A Storytelling Revival on the Farm 39
What are we going to make better today? 43
She's the Wind, She's Nebraska 51
Farm Bike Tires 55
In the Heartland? 59
She's Nebraska 63
Don't do what Mother Nature will do for Free 67
Spanish Teacher, Market Gardener, and Mexico Traveler 71
The Great Mauck Relay Cropping Reset 77
A Better Way to Farm 83
We Would be Lost Without Him 89
A Common Sense, Informed Passion for Soil Health 97
Thank You for Coming Home 103
His Name is Gail – The Recovering Conventional Farmer 111
Farm Foreclosures and Legacy 121
Homeland Ties 125
My God, My Family, and My Art 129
Regenerative Agriculture Holds Promise for Next Generation 133
Urban Farming a Labor of Love 137
Circle of Friends for Soil Health 143
A Lot of Love and Nip and Tuck 147
The Lutheran Institute of Regenerative Agriculture 155

Where there's a Will, there's a McCoy 161
A Name Synonymous with Soil: Dr. Ray Ward 167
Umatilla Tribal Members Regenerating Soils and Community 173
Rolling T's Custom Kitchen 177
The Fairest in the Land: Magic Valley Potatoes 183
Observational Agriculture 189
North Star Dreams 195
Regenerating for the Next Generation 203
Born to Farm, Born to Live 209

Foreword

Hope Stories are an effort of the Graze Master Group to bring real rural stories to life. These stories are messages to the future from voices we admire who are willing to look at the rural reality for what it is and make changes that balance nature and profitability on their farms and ranches. These salt of the earth people are displaying the leadership and courage so desperately needed to implement the solutions we need to build the soil and community.

What is the Graze Master Group?

Graze Master Group partners have an inherent understanding of the serious issues facing farms, ranches, agribusinesses, the greater community, and the natural world we depend on for sustenance and all life. Each and every one of our partners are doing something constructive to solve problems and to design solutions in the areas they are conducting business: farming, ranching, producing products, designing equipment, building community, serving as civic leaders, and more.

We're entrepreneurs, innovators, farmers, ranchers, global business leaders, optimists, realists, thinkers, and doers who are driven by education and making a positive impact as we build upon the strong agrarian foundation that we all share worldwide. Our soil, water, and natural resources need saving and renewing. We are confident we have the human resources within our group and the greater Graze Master Group network to make a positive and profitable difference for the future.

The plains have been a place of both pain and promise. We are the descendants of families who have experienced both of those things. Combined, all these stories are written to the future, a future we hope and pray our descendants will see if we get this right.

Thank you for taking this journey with us. Let's not give up – hope.

Kerry Hoffschneider and Del Ficke
Co-founders of the Graze Master Group
www.grazemastergroup.com

To My Future Generations

KERRY HOFFSCHNEIDER | JULY 30, 2022

A LETTER BY DEL FICKE
DICTATED AND EDITED BY KERRY HOFFSCHNEIDER

FROM LEFT, HAYDEN, ALYSSA, AUSTIN, OLIVIA, ATTLEY, BRENDA, DEL, AND EMILY FICKE.

In 1860, Johann Ficke made the trip from Germany to settle in the United States. Just nine years later, after first arriving in Wisconsin, he found a beautiful spot a mile west of Pleasant Dale, Neb. to homestead and begin the labors that have become our family's legacy. In 1888, Johann purchased the farm I grew up on for my great-grandfather H.F.

and his wife Annette when they got married. H.F. and Annette had four sons and two daughters – my grandpa Adolph, Frank, Fred, Hank, Mary, and Helen. Adolph and Lana had three children – Clifford (who tragically died at the age of three), my father Kenneth, and a daughter Ellen.

To this day, we are farmers and cattlemen – that is the core of our family's agricultural history. However, at the center of the story is family – we all live very close to one another. My sisters Janet, Rhonda, and Jolene live within a section of my wife Brenda and our daughter Emily. My mother, Beverly, lives just across the lawn right next to our house. I am also so proud to say that my son Austin, his wife Alyssa, and their children Attley, Hayden, Olivia, and Kenneth (K.C.), live in the farmhouse right next to us. Needless to say, my heart bursts with the blessing of generations of Fickes living here today.

However, while genealogies are important, I write this letter to those who will come far after I am gone in order that you better understand the realities of carrying on a true family farming operation – the key is the family. This personal family story truly begins with my father Kenneth who was always putting himself aside, so we would have a better life. His secret was simple – a life-long commitment to clearly communicating to all of us how we were the most essential part of keeping the farm going. We were his legacy, not the land and the livestock, but rather the family he loved so much.

In the early 80s, dad and mom told my sisters and me to come around the table. They had a plan and we were part of the plan. It was fair and equitable in that it was based on each of our level of involvement in the farming operation. There were no issues because we were all there to ask questions and we respected what they were saying because it was coming from our mom and dad's mouths, not a piece of paper after they were gone. Their hearts and minds were in front of us, sharing their dreams and desires. As siblings, there was no going back on that because we all loved each other, respected one another, and trusted their plans were what was best.

Dad and mom set up everything as a Life Estate. In our case, this means the land was deeded to all of us kids and as our parents they retained life use of it. They agreed to pay all expenses and get all the income. For example, my father has since passed away, so right now my mom rents all the land to me and she pays taxes and gets the cash rent income. I am paying for land that is already deeded to me. But, that's okay, because the land has always been protected and because as a family we have verbally talked this through and clearly understand the intended purposes of this type of arrangement.

Constant change and passing down responsibility has been the difference maker in our family. Growing up, my father sent me all over the country to learn about cattle and agriculture. When I was 20 years old at Thanksgiving my dad announced to everyone, "Del will be in charge of the farming operation starting tomorrow morning." He hadn't told me that prior to the public announcement. But, I understand why now. My dad did not want his son not understanding how every part of the operation worked at a young age. He would often bring up stories of our neighbors with sons who were 50 to 80 years old and had no clue when the father passed away how to run the farm.

My father's decision to hand over the reins early to me doesn't mean that it didn't come without a lot of stress at times. However, the key factor was that he was alive to provide the guidance and allow me to make the decisions. He ultimately watched me make a lot of mistakes and achieve some successes. However, there was hands-down no more co-signing of notes. It was my business to run – profits and losses.

I built our farming operation to 7,000 acres of farmland and pastures for Ficke Cattle Company. I did this through relationship building and learning to adopt new practices to create more efficiencies. One of those practices was no-till. In 1987, I started no-tilling. For one growing season my dad would not talk to me about the crops that he was so dismayed about planting into the weeds and stalks. It turned out that first year of no-tilling was a very dry year. On dad's tilled acres the yields suffered. However, on my end, the no-till acres doubled in production over his tilled acres. Needless to say, dad was a no-till fan after that.

In 1999, things dramatically changed again and needed to. I believe that when my back blew out that year, God was sending me a message about the future and what really matters about family farming. The farm boy was forced to re-think his life. I went to college because I couldn't physically farm that many acres and stay alive. During college, I was still managing all 7,000 acres. Then I decided to offer the farming opportunity to my nephews – Matt and Ryan. In turn, I took a position managing a medical clinic in Lincoln, Neb. while still maintaining my cow herd.

Agriculture was always in my heart though and I have been blessed to see agriculture from so many points of view. Because of my experiences both on and off the farm, I have been inspired to embark on a new journey. Today, I am back home running an approximately 600-acre farm that I rent from my mom who continues to have life use. My goal is to restore and improve the soils back to the way God intended. A couple years ago we started implementing cover crops on our operation. We are also taking row-crop acres and putting them into season-long cover crop grazing scenarios and ensuring our native pastures are performing at their maximum potential.

We have trademarked our composite breed of cattle – Graze Master Genetics® that are suited for 100 percent forage-based programs. I have also consulted across the country on cattle and transitioning farms and ranches in a more holistic manner. My passion is taking what I have learned and helping others learn from my mistakes and successes along the way.

Most importantly, I feel like we are doing the right things again. We are enjoying the smell of sweet clover and alfalfa. We have the Hendl family nearby now, providing bees and producing honey that in turn gives us healthier crops and pastures. There are a host of rewarding transformations taking place.

The farm is full of more birds than ever. I carry around a bird book, so I can identify them. I also carry a range book and a cover crop guide, so I can identify the new plants coming up through the soil. We are also not irrigated so water conservation issues are real and top-of-mind every day.

Improving the environment on this farm is a top goal. We have decreased the use of chemicals and synthetic fertilizers by 95 percent on our pastures. It's always about building up the soil and retaining the water. We also want to continue to make our farm a place where all our neighbors both rural and urban are welcome and can gain educational opportunities.

My Grandpa Adolph and my father's voice are a constant companion with me. Both were big on community and neighbors. Grandpa Adolph said, "The day the horses left, and the tractor came, was the day we replaced community with competition." Grandpa would constantly talk with me about the way we were doing things on the farm, and he didn't think things were going the right way. He was anti too much government and anti the overreach of corporations into farming and livestock. Grandpa Adolph certainly helped me be more discerning about what is being "sold" to the typical farmer – everything from equipment to chemicals. There's a lot of propaganda about what we really "need" and a lot more wisdom needed to actually make those decisions about what we need.

Like the generations before me, the family is the most important part of the farm. It is their talents and gifts that are the most precious resources. The land must be worked for and is not guaranteed; however, the creativity of the next generation can keep the farm and Ficke Cattle Company going with new ideas and dreams. Thirty years from now I want to be remembered for always doing the right thing. I want to be known for doing things the way God intended. Work must mean something through the generations. There must be integrity – with your community, family, and the environment.

Hell's Half Acre

KERRY HOFFSCHNEIDER | APRIL 6, 2021

AUSTIN FICKE AND HIS GRANDPA KENNETH FICKE.

Del Ficke said his dad, Kenneth, sometimes referred to their eastern Nebraska dryland farm and ranch as "Hell's Half Acre."

"Life was good on 'Hell's Half Acre' though," said Del Ficke. "During my early years, dad shielded me from the things he did not want me around. He helped get me educated in different ways of agriculture and sent me all over the country on bus tours with his business friends who were leaders in our community."

Then the 1980s hit.

"I thought we were rolling with our registered Herefords and we still were, but I remember sitting in the living room with my dad when he said, 'Well, I don't know what's all going to take place. It seems we are losing a lot of equity and interest is going up and guys have already started selling some stuff off. I think the talk is coming from our banker.'"

"I said, 'Dad our banker was just out here at our Hereford event, just praising us about how we are doing,'" Ficke recalled. "Then everything changed. It seemed like overnight. My dad did not have his neck stuck out like some guys did financially – but any amount of debt was taxing on him."

"We paid our debt back," he went on. "Dad did not have to look over his shoulder like a lot of guys did in the 1980s."

While the times were difficult, it was during the 1980s Farm Crisis when Ficke said he began to learn the meaning of "the Golden Rule" on "Hell's Half Acre," "Everyone stopped to see my dad – setting on the back steps or at the kitchen table. They weren't there to console him. They were asking him for advice. It was a whole new territory for everyone, and people were still coming together back then."

"Many people died in that deal. Many people died and kept living," he said soberly about the lasting impacts of the 1980s.

Life kept on at the more fondly referred to – Ficke Cattle Company, where Ficke still resides today along with the now seventh generation being raised at the place his father put under his management in his early twenties. Located in the rolling prairie hills, Del and his father's first love were the cows – farming was just a necessity.

"That picture of my dad with the combine and my son Austin is the day we sold it. We sold a 35-year-old combine and bought a 25-year-old combine – a 1977 John Deere 6600 diesel," he said. "I remember exactly what my dad told Austin that day, 'I hope you never have to run one of these damn things.'"

Kenneth and his relationship with machines.

"Yes, he hated them. I can't really repeat any of what he said about machines. There was nothing gentle about his tongue-lashing of equipment," Ficke admitted.

"Dad preferred cows and so did I. He basically gave his life making sure those cows were well taken care of – in a lot of ways, he was doing things that really didn't need to be done. 'There will come a time when these cows have to take care of themselves,' he would say," Ficke recalled.

"So, one day I told him, 'Let's make that time today,'" Ficke said matter-of-factly.

That's exactly what Ficke did – changed the way he did things, "I watched my dad, a perfectionist, fight the farm and work cows and make it hard with a lot of industrialized ag 'advice.' When I started making changes, he couldn't get enough of seeing that. We were defying the odds that everyone was saying. I am glad he could witness a part of what we were changing before he died."

Ficke went from several thousand acres to less that 600 acres and became more profitable managing less and focusing on soil health and working in tune with nature far more. Some of the ways he has changed is by:

> Reducing chemicals in pastureland by 95 percent with controlled grazing.

> Inter-seeding pastures with legumes that will produce the nitrogen needed so there is no longer a need for commercial fertilizer.

> Taking highly erodible cropland out of corn production and putting it into grazing situations to help return the soil closer to its original potential.

> Marketing Ficke Cattle Company beef directly to his community. His family is proud to know every, single customer by name.

Welcoming the community – consumers of food – to come out and visit a working farm and to enjoy God's great creation.

Most importantly, they are focusing on including the next generation. Del, his wife Brenda, daughter Emily, son Austin and his wife Alyssa along with their granddaughters and grandson – Attley, Hayden, Olivia, and Kenneth are all at the heart of his motivations each day.

Before the 1980s hit, Ficke said his father enjoyed farming more. He attributed the change to the stress that weighed upon relationships in the community, "I think my dad enjoyed most everything in agriculture before then – but then it just got to him because it was shocking to go through that – the remnants of that shock are still reverberating through the countryside today. Our old mailman from back then said after the 80s hit, 'The farmers went from falling out of the pickup or tractor to wave at you, to barely acknowledging that someone was waving at them.'"

"I would like to put the word 'relations' back into 'relationships,'" Ficke said. "When I was a kid, it was about a handshake and looking a man in his eyes. Your word was your word."

"Dad did not raise me to back down when I knew a situation wasn't right," Ficke said. "I am expecting to get my nose bloodied a few times in the fight when it comes to addressing some of the serious issues going on in agriculture. I was able to see many of the towns and communities vibrant that are now suffering. If we get the soil right again, everything else gets better – from livestock to crops and community."

"Agriculture has to seek a harmonious relationship between man, beast and nature," he said in closing. "We can talk all day about how 'good it used to be' or 'how it should have been.' In its current state, agriculture is like that house for sale that says, 'excellent fixer-upper.' We've got a hell of a lot of fixing to do, but I know we can do it because I have seen the positive results from making changes at Ficke Cattle Company and I am seeing others see a better way too."

The Guiding Star on Our Old Shed

KERRY HOFFSCHNEIDER | JANUARY 3, 2024

When I take the trash out after supper and the moon is already out, I walk the path that leads me to the blue snowflake beaming from the side of the old building door facing north on the farm.

A north snowflake star, she has to be so cold hanging there manning her post with such calm dignity. But beam on she does. A guiding light caught in-between old times and new times. Yes indeed, even though it's hard and frigid some days, this one was born to shine through the eons of time.

It's just so pretty to stand there under the deep blue sky and the stars above warming the night with their glow and just bask in the magic of the moment. Such a loving light she is, hugging the cracked paint of the sliding door. It's as if she's the steering wheel at the helm of a ship, sailing that old building forward into times yet to be seen. I can almost hear the creaking of the building bend with the winds as the snowflake desperately shines on to bring time forward.

To no avail though, there's just no sailing the old building forever ahead. She likes to remain firm and set on her foundation. We too are like that. We too will wear out, grow tired, and windswept like she is, torn between the dance of the old ways and the world always spiraling into something new. There's no denying we'll all be facing the light at the end of the tunnel one day too.

So very full of life's glow the snowflake light makes what may seem undesirable to some, desirable, really beautiful I think. I really do think she's perfect, hanging on chipped paint and all.

I love that old building most of all.

No, I wouldn't want the snowflake star hung on anything new. She's perfect there, holding onto the fading, peeling paint entryway of another time. I am alive, but also gradually fading like that as well. It won't be long, and I will have plenty more creases pressed into my body from time passing through me too.

We all need to grow older with new "starflakes" glowing love upon us. Maybe they will be grand babies. Maybe just the magic of a loving moment in a day. Maybe just reaching a near perfect moment to stand there and appreciate the glow of it all.

That's the hope isn't it? The hope is to make it through as long as we can. Held together by undeserved grace, forgiveness, and all sorts of warm love. That's what the world really needs now. That sort of forever love. A little snowflake on the side of an old cracked door showed me that.

Yes, she shines, that little loving snowflake, bracing the cold she pushes through with her light. She warms the night and reminds me, there's plenty of cracks to maneuver through in life, but love in all its forms will always make it. Love shines in the darkest nights. Love will lead us to the forever light.

"To realize one's destiny is a person's only obligation."

Kerry Hoffschneider | October 30, 2023

Luke has a book, *The Alchemist*, by Paulo Coelho. On the back cover it reads, "To realize one's destiny is a person's only obligation."

"Mom, have you read *The Alchemist*?" he asked, passing through the kitchen as I stood at the sink scrubbing a muffin pan. A frustrating task of swirling, scrubbing, "spongery" drudgery.

As my mind and intellect intersects with the children's minds and happenings of their lives, I consider the far-reaching journey of my own mind and how the kitchen sink is so very far away from the dreams my thoughts take me to.

I stand there in their lives, growing up speedily before me, practicing one act play lines with them, looking at school papers, and giggling at Caroline's very normal pre-teen attitude. And yet, here I am, their mother and also dreaming of seeing earth from space one day, watching the costs of private space flights, and reading about the Apollo 11 crew. Yes, I read countless books and articles, scribble down my passing thoughts, and sometimes drive or fly away to watch the lightbulbs go on in farmers' minds across the nation as they realize their soils are dying, water is depleted/polluted, and they need new life breathed into their land, heart, and intellect.

Yes, new life we all need. A breath of fresh, informed air would do us all good. A series of deep breaths, too.

Caroline hollers from the west side of the farmhouse, "Look at the sunset, mom."

I run out, dishtowel in hand, the old-fashioned white kind that dries pots and pans better than the rest. The clothes dryer also goes off. But we have a minute there together at the west window and I tell her it's beautiful, "So beautiful, Caroline. You're so right. One worth stopping for."

The wind that beats Nebraskans most days slows to an evening calm. I shut the kitchen lights off, only the one glowing fixture over the sink remains. I look at the faucet, considering how easily water pours from it. I feel the finiteness of the precious water as I rinse my hands once more. I consider what's in store as I peer out eastward. Way over there somewhere is New York City.

They will all need a drink, too, forever, I think to myself. New Yorker neighbors far to the east and York, Nebraska neighbors just a few minutes to the west all share that common denominator; they need water to live.

The dryer buzzer hums to silence. I decide to leave that last load to fold in the morning. I go upstairs to draw a bath. More water usage to consider. Everywhere I turn I am reminded.

I sink into the tub and write these words. I think about how swiftly time is running out. I think about the children, their lives, their dreams, and my dreams. Dreams directly connected to every drop of water. The world's dreams are connected to that water, too.

I cherish these autumn moments, arranging pumpkins on the porch Caroline grew next to her pigs this summer. The fall decor pleases me. It's symbolic, an expression of gratitude for the green growing portion year.

It's the transition time between harvest, then relentless cold, then the warm light of life again. I can almost hear the seeds settling in their piles for a long winter's rest. I overhear the whispers of chilly roots dreaming and hoping for spring to come again. The worms, insects, and microbes scurry to warm nooks and crannies of soil to live and hibernate. The water braces itself for the big freeze.

After my bath, I sort through the coat closet and bring last year's winter coats out. I hold them up and shake the stale air from them. They still fit. They'll do.

But what will we do? I ask myself. The house completely silent now with sleepers. Everyone but me, my book, my prayers, and my heart beating. I drink a glass of water. I think of the significance of it. I think of the quote on Luke's book: "To realize one's destiny is a person's only obligation."

I am obligated to a purpose. This water beneath me, soaking through the spongy layers of the aquifer as I wring out my kitchen sponge. We need to treasure this purpose, protect it, renew it. There are so many more mouths that need a drink beyond the four living here in a farmhouse.

I quietly turn to the stairway, and pull shut the farmhouse door to the upstairs. I climb with my worries and dreams intact. I lean back on the bed, and think of that trip one day I dream of to view earth from space. I pray it's still a blue planet by then. A fresh water rich planet.

If we could only see the treasure before us standing here right now. Water, more precious than gold. We cannot eat money, yet we act like it. My head hits the pillow, but I won't fully rest until I have breathed my last breath trying to inform a world disconnected from the soil, precious water, and itself.

I am trying to meet my obligations with purpose. I will try, Luke. I will.

York County Fair

Kerry Hoffschneider | August 8, 2023

There were new boots at the York County Fair. I can tell you there were because I was just there. I remember the county fair well. Different times. I wasn't allowed to stray too far from my parents' side in those days. I guess you could say I was an observer back then, much like today. For various reasons, we weren't a 4-H family. I didn't even do FFA. That is why it was such a big deal for me when I earned my Honorary State FFA Degree as a professional adult.

I was working for a global seed company then. A global seed company started by Henry A. Wallace, way back when farmers across the land were marveling about the wonders of hybrid corn. I still have a necklace, a simple one I picked up at some department store, with a cheap silver infinity symbol swinging between two chains. The same infinity symbol on the original Pioneer® Seed bags. But while the symbol represents forever, things certainly changed in the seed industry. They changed like the changes I saw at the fair.

Another hybrid corn leader to know about was Mr. Roswell Garst, the Coon Rapids, Iowa farmer who didn't let the Cold War stop him from inviting Soviet Premier Nikita Khrushchev to his farm. Garst knew what a full or empty stomach meant to a world that never seems to want to cease the wars. He also knew the great wealth potential ahead and he wasn't going to let that opportunity pass him by.

Growing up I knew my only opportunities in agriculture would be through pursuing a higher education. I knew because I watched the farms around me continue to consolidate and I also listened very closely to the adults around me. I listened to talk about the seemingly inevitable trends, that the fence rows and shelter belts were completely on their way out. It was just the way it was going to be, fewer farms and more rows of corn. Still, the highest form of nutrition is within the four-legged beast that is by God's design, made to graze on forages and grass. Once wild, in herds, they were a mobile and highly efficient creator of calories from a natural cycle. Since then, many have been domesticated and reduced down to a feeding trough.

I spent nearly all my life learning the reasons there were insiders and outsiders in agriculture the world over. Coming home to the county fair now seems like slipping through a wrinkle in time. A wrinkle like the ones I see on faces of families I thought would be raising livestock forever. Forever, like that infinity symbol on a sack of seed. The only thing that guarantees forever on the farm is the pursuit of one's passions in action. A pursuit I am on, to help people see these farms can go on, and there can be even more of them. But it's going to take something new to get there. It's going to take being proud of something that really matters and the wisdom of knowing that it's not yield and technology. It's people and precious natural resources.

Our very lives depend on our ability to see the problems at hand and to change. The very soil beneath our feet and water we can't drink is dying for us to figure this out.

In my favorite novel of all time, Willa Cather's *O' Pioneers*, the heroine Alexandra Bergstrom says this, "The land belongs to the future, Carl; that's the way it seems to me. How many of the names on the county clerk's plat will be there in fifty years? I might as well try to will the sunset over there to my brother's children. We come and go, but the land is always here. And the people who love it and understand it are the people who own it – for a little while."

All the people who own it for a little while. That little while is perhaps halfway near its end for me. Tomorrow is promised to no one, not even the next second. I heard someone say this midway point in life was, "halfway to harvest time." The harvest is plentiful, but the workers are few. We need new cowboy and cowgirl boots, more workers, more planners and dreamers, more people, that's what will transform the current farms and envision more of them.

I think that's a rightful place to place our prairie pride in, the potential of people, people on the outside looking in with so much to give and people on the inside with so much to give and so much to learn. The next generation of true pioneers that surpasses any infinity symbol, is rooted in a people-centered, not self-centered agriculture that has the wisdom to understand what really has value forever. What really has value is the heart in the heartland. That's where we start so the land can be fruitful again.

The John Deere 630

Kerry Hoffschneider | July 29, 2023

If you could push the clutch back on a John Deere 630 and keep it there at just the right speed so the irrigation pipe could be laid out without starting and stopping over and over again, there was a summer job just for you on an irrigated York County Nebraska farm.

I was about five years old when I tried my very darnedest to use my entire body to lean in and make that pesky PTO clutch go and then yanked it back with all my might to make it stop. But often my attempts were to no avail.

I was far more adept at maneuvering the 630 forward when the pipe rack was empty, and I was driving the tractor full speed ahead down the center of Road P towards home. My dad stood next to me while I was perched on the bright yellow tractor seat, both hands on the wheel, feeling free as a bird.

Yes, I was basking in over-confidence during that straight arrow drive until it was time to turn into the farmyard. As we approached the corner, I would twist my neck around to see if dad was going to help. But it was always full steam ahead and I was certain I would go careening into the honey locust trees that lined the gravel driveway. Dad was at ease though, taking gulps of iced tea from the thermos while one hand rested on the arm of my tractor seat.

Finally, just in the nick of time, he slowed us down and I would hear him yelling over the loud, puffing, putt-putt-putting engine. "Keep it wide, Kerry," he would say as I turned and arrived safely south of the white barn where we stacked the pipe in two gray metal piles. Or, I should say, more often than not, (where my sister stacked pipe with dad) while I sang into the long, cylindrical echoing "microphones." I would also take my hand and scoop out the fine sediment that settled on the base of each end of pipe after the last pools of water dried, water we were pumping from deep within the aquifer to irrigate rows of Golden Harvest milo and Pioneer Hybrid corn.

Yes, I soon learned that monotonous tractor driving wasn't for me. While my older sister was quick to prove her prowess at backing up machines and hitching up implements, my goal was to prove I couldn't, so I didn't have to. After being chastised time and again for not being able to yank back or push forward the wobbly iron rod, one day I just decided to make my way to the second step of the 630 with those Lego-looking holes, jumped far down onto the dusty trail, and ran away free, weeeeeee!

The 630 kept purring away on its own at a few miles per hour (if that even). Dad quickly noticed my absence and went running for the open-air tractor as two narrow tires veered towards the metal pipe, lined up neatly next to the crops. Just in time, he was able to bring the 630 to a stop. And, just in time, I was sprinting out of ear shot, too far away to hear any of the hollering.

So yes, that was the day I walked away from the John Deere machine operator job and didn't look back. I had better things to do anyway, with my fort in the trees planted and watered by hand by my grandfather. The fort was in the pasture where the neighbor's cows grazed. There was also my raft to build. I was certain I could set sail on the irrigation pond one day. Peering out at the mini body of water, I would sing Frank Sinatra's hit, "Start Spreading the News … New York, New York." I dreamed of heading towards Upper New York Bay as I waved at the Statue of Liberty on Liberty Island. I mean, if I could make it there, I could make it anywhere, right?

But there were always cows to converse with calling me back home or kittens to pull from between hot and scratchy hay bales in the barn. The baby kitties were as scratchy as the bales with their tiny, razor-sharp claws wedged into my flesh through my cotton "Air Force Academy" t-shirt. But soon they were meowing all over the place and one couldn't help but cuddle the little furry balls with four legs despite their poky paws.

No, machines weren't meant for me. But the farm was, the nature part, and the joy of seeing my Grandma Ruth's green boat of a car pulling in to get her gardening done or to take her granddaughters to her apartment in York for a weekend stay. I can still see the trunk open and her seed packets ready to go. She was always dressed neat as a pin, even to garden. She would even wear stiff, body-shaping undergarments under her garden clothes and the whole bit, sometimes with curlers in her hair and a sheer green scarf wrapped around them.

She always had her purse with a tube of Merle Norman lipstick inside. I always liked to grab a piece of Doublemint gum and her car keys. I would take them and pretend my hand-me-down boy's yellow dirt bike with a black banana seat was a car. I drove around to the milk house, machine shed, and other farm buildings, pretending I was in (you guessed it) New York City.

Yes, I sure gave that John Deere 630 an honest try. But I couldn't help it. I was made to be on the move on foot or bicycle. I have been on that move ever since. Still, I learned something there, something about life. I learned about the warm refuge of a grandmother's love. I heard her stories about the family of 13 she grew up in while we snapped green beans and pushed tiny peas into old ice cream buckets from juicy pods. We also pitted cherries, picked apples, and played catch in the backyard. We wore stiff jeans from the clothesline and headed to the neighbor's dairy to bottle feed the baby calves. Life was work and adventures, too.

Inside there were chores to be done and children to be cared for. There were kids all around, in fact, that I babysat. Work always came first and then play. There wasn't a dishwasher in the early days and only five channels on the television. I loved weekends at grandma's because she let us stay up to watch Saturday Night Live when Chevy Chase and the cast inspired me to make up my own comedy skits.

I learned how to make hamburger gravy in the cast iron skillet. I also learned the art of casting your cares away on the long walks my grandma would take. Long walks I take during just about every sunrise to this day.

There were very tough times there, but there were good times, too. I learned I wasn't a tractor driver. I was an explorer. I had too many questions for everyone and was always looking around the bend. Still, the farm is where that exploration began, that deep connection to what is really real.

You learn a lot on a farm. Yes, you really do. I learned tractor driving wasn't for me, but the open road is. I also learned a lot about living and dying on the farm. Those who know, just know. They are the kind of lessons the world needs right about now. The kind of lessons that would straighten a lot of things out. Lessons I'll never forget.

Photo courtesy of my sister Jenny. I love her so much and she was absolutely the best tractor driver in the family.

These Country Roads

KERRY HOFFSCHNEIDER | FEBRUARY 25, 2023

A NEBRASKA COUNTRY ROAD.

These country roads.
They're something aren't they?
The last promise of a promise. The last hope of hopes.
As they grow old, we do too.
We ought to believe in something more than them though, so we can make something of them.

This is our last-ditch effort. As ditches get plowed under, we will too.

These country roads.

They weren't here forever.

They came here after the buffalo and countless people who were driven out by a criminal, inhumane plan.

They came after trains and the Homestead Act.

They are a manufactured relic we try and keep up.

They became the stuff of coffee shop talk – simplified into the subjects of not enough gravel or too much.

But maintaining country roads today and maintaining them for generations is a far deeper conversation. Yes, a far bigger one. That's probably why we talk about the former and not the latter more often.

Because today we just need to get to town or keep our tractors, trucks, and combines heading down the road.

The tomorrows that seem so far away are unfolding though upon these country roads. Who will actually be living alongside them is up for grabs – land grabs today, and a host of unknown land grabs that will happen in countless tomorrows.

So much has become extinct since their fruition in the countryside. I don't always think we consider ourselves caught up in the same process.

But we are in the same story of survival, revival, or a forever downward spiral.

Yes, these country roads have a story to tell.

It's our story of some successes and also the same ol' story of wearing down the same paths too often and not taking the road less traveled often enough.

These country roads are a network of history, crisscrossing a continent that has been spinning its wheels from the start.

Some will continue to lead somewhere, others will lead to what there once was.

Tales they once told will be forgotten and new tales will emerge and we'll wonder what happened or we'll make things happen.

Like it or not, these roads are mirrors.

Mirages sometimes, yet always the truth.

All the time, these country roads, even the ones forgotten, are what started this nation.

They hold ghosts of pride and of promise that need to learn from their triumphs and mistakes.

It's where we're headed – if where we are, are these country roads.

Like it or not. We're going where they are or where we direct them to.

These country roads.

The end.

Or, the beginning of something even better. We choose.

Just up the road...

KERRY HOFFSCHNEIDER | OCTOBER 26, 2022

A NEBRASKA COUNTRY ROAD IN MY CORNER OF THE BIG, BEAUTIFUL WORLD.

Just up the road I watch the changing leaves lining a country mile throughout the seasons. It's a road I've taken thousands of times by now.

Just up the road further north is where my life began, and I remember packing boxes when I was very young for the move our old farmhouse was making. The orchard was gone in the front yard, and we were moving the house closer to the road. The road where my brother and his family are living today. I am so happy about that house full of life thriving along the country road.

Just up the road north of there is the cemetery where mom was buried not long after she decorated just about every room of our house with wallpaper and hosted card party in the basement. She covered one of the card tables with cheetah print contact paper and I will never forget it.

Just up the road even further north and east of there is Thayer, Neb. where our church, Zion Lutheran, used to sit and has since been moved just up the road clear back south to Wessels Living History Farm outside York, Neb.

Just up the road on I-80 is the State Capitol, where I once headed to work at a seed company and learned about ag business on a global scale and who had sights on the land and its bounty far from the roads I knew and far from the pickup truck we used to load with bags of seed.

Just up the road heading south from York, Neb. is Plainview, Texas, where I saw the sorghum and cotton fields and many pivots running dry. Water issues facing many roads here and afar cause me to lose sleep at night.

Head even further south down the road and you'll find a committed and hardworking group of migrant workers with dreams of their own in the fields, harvesting the food we all consume and doing work many of us won't do.

Now let's go east down some roads not far from the Atlantic ocean, where many of our European ancestors arrived after hellish ship rides, dragging their belongings in cargo trunks behind them, looking for work, maybe heading to farm, maybe going to the city, maybe just hanging on for dear life.

Come with me on the Oregon Trail, walk with me if you would to that smoke in the distance, see that Pawnee mother holding her sleeping baby. Look into her eyes and see how very much the same we truly are.

Travel with me on roads further back to the Battle of Little Big Horn, to Arlington Cemetery and the race riots in Omaha and Memphis.

Consider with me how human beings fighting on seemingly opposing sides are fighting for the same thing – freedom, a right to be seen as fully human, and a right to live out their lives.

Just up the road out here where I live, there are fewer neighbors than there used to be and fewer trees and that's why I love the remaining few groves so very much. The trees are like neighbors to me too and will outlive us all.

Maybe you're just up the road, living a peaceful day, making your coffee, complaining about work, holding your grandchild, owning a car, with plenty of food to eat and thankful for it all. All the while, just up the road on a far-off road, someone else is getting bombed, displaced, starving, and disillusioned by it all.

Just up the road next door, there's suffering too, depression, loneliness, sickness, and worst – hopelessness.

Roads take us to places known and unknown and back home. I've always loved the open roads the most and even as a child wondered about why we had all the fences, gates, walls, and borders. I even often wondered what road really led to home. "Earth," I'd say to my friends. "That's where I am from. Earth."

Just up the road is a neighbor in need. If we start changing things there, we change the quality and ease of the travel on life's road for everyone.

So, see you later, and hopefully soon, just up some country road or somewhere in-between. Enjoy your road, wherever it may go, and may you always find deep meaning in your travels and arrive safely wherever you feel most at home.

SEEDS - Published on Tuesday, Oct. 25 in the York News-Times.

A Storytelling Revival on the Farm

Kerry Hoffschneider | June 8, 2022

Four years old in 1980, barefoot on a Nebraska farm, riding my bike.

The quietness of night fell around me in the farmhouse and there I was, left listening to my thoughts. I took a deep breath after heading to tuck my restless daughter in for the third time. "It's okay, I've been restless, too," I thought to myself as I crept out of her room and whispered, "Jesus loves you and mama, too."

Leaning back against the headboard of the bed, I reflected upon life on the "modern farm." A pillow covered with a quilted sham became my desk for my writing paper, a hand-me-down from Luke. He had given me a stack of spiral notebooks on the last day of school. "I'm done with these," he said in his orderly manner. "But there's still empty paper left. You can have them." So, I took them from him and slid them under my already healthy pile of scrap paper I use to keep my lists of grocery items and to-do notes I am constantly writing to myself.

The night continued falling around my thoughts, and on my notebook, the same type of notebook I was writing in about 38 years ago. Since then, many of those words have been burned – too dark and confusing for anyone to come across. Still, I haven't stopped trying to get the words out about the painfully slow death and ever so slow revival of the nation's family farms. The personal pain of losing a mother, the pain of family members who faded away from our lives afterwards, the pain of unanswered questions left behind by more farming to do and the to-do list that forever marches on.

I know where I learned to keep up with tasks and lose myself. The "family farm" taught me that. The same "family farm" among many others that also lost moms in the 1980s, not to death, but to jobs they were forced to take because the bank was putting the pressure on. There were bills to pay and the noose of health insurance began dragging them away from home. Many know what I'm talking about. Decisions made out of fear in desperate times. Decisions that changed lives forever literally overnight.

We were the farm kids watching our parents at waist level. We were feeling what was going on. We knew what was leaving the farm. We watched mom pack her lunch and distant dads. We knew about short tempers and so much work to do.

We also knew about pick-up basketball games on cement slabs by old barns and garages. We knew about playing outdoors. And, we also knew all too well the harsh lyrics from John Mellencamp songs. Yes, we knew about those "400 empty acres" that used to be a lot of neighbors' farms. We also tried to read minds. We tried to make out what was being said in the whispers and the deafening silence too.

We were the "latch key" generation trying to find meaning on the farm while what really made the "family farm" was leaving – the family itself. First were the dads just trying to keep it together, then moms to work, then kids to their rooms and off to big colleges that consumed them. We were growing up too fast and not at all at the same time. We felt guilty and we didn't know all the reasons why.

On one hand we longed to be wild as ever, and on the other hand we longed to live the lives our grandparents had, listening to their stories of simpler times. But really, nothing had ever been simple on the farm. What had been better was the genuine connection between neighbors. The natural resources – when the West Blue River was really blue. When the soil was far richer with organic matter. When the apples falling from trees were more nutrient dense. When there was time for more fishing.

I believe we all suffer from at least a touch of "ag-PTSD (post-traumatic stress disorder)." A division has occurred and into "two houses" agriculture now stands. We're at war within ourselves and in competition with the last of our neighbors. We're the children of the 80s, or at least we were within earshot of the Farm Crisis that we've conveniently swept under kitchen tables we gather around fewer and fewer times.

I'm crawling out from under the kitchen table now, word by word. The future needs our stories as sordid as some can get. The future also needs more family farms. We can get there by sharing. It's as hard and simple as that. I get it. I live it, and many of you do too. We can start by writing down or speaking a single word. As night falls on the farm, a new dawn can also rise and shine on the family farm's future if we clearly understand the past. We need a revival of authentic storytelling on the farm. I am going to start. Maybe you can too. Maybe those words can heal. Maybe there is hope. I think so. I really do.

What are we going to make better today?

Kerry Hoffschneider | July 15, 2022

Several years ago, I learned something new about agriculture. The agriculture I had written about for more than a decade prior to learning the good news about farmers and ranchers finding a better way. I was renewed with hope. It was like this good news has been held from us or even censored. I wanted to learn why.

Now it has been nearly 20 years of professionally and personally cleaving myself to the topics infiltrating and inspiring all things around agriculture. The topics that have literally defined every aspect of my life. My choice. Maybe my destiny. Maybe my curse. For whatever reason, there's no looking back.

Now I am absolutely confident of this: the nation and world can heal if one farm and ranch at a time makes some changes that better their own lives and the lives of others. Making these changes will also afford more people opportunities to be fruitful from the land. Right now, we're looking to others (the government, grandparents, businesses and institutions) to do this for us. However, I am calling out to people everywhere passionate about the future of our sustenance, and screaming this from the rooftops: we're going to have to cooperate and do this ourselves.

At one ignorant point during my "blinders completely on" early journalism, public relations, and farm advocacy career, I wrote glowing stories about an agriculture that had actually run amok in many areas.

I wanted to believe in the glossy propaganda promising to "feed the world."

I wanted to believe ag corporations and land grant universities were all pristine in their pursuit to do what's best for the ol' people down on the farm.

As farm families worked hard to find a firm footing on shaky ground across the nation, some of the rural children growing up when I did in the late 1970s, 80s and 90s, sought affirmation and attention from some of the most wretched, depraved scenarios that my soul is not yet prepared to share.

If you know what I mean, you also know how desperate we were to find "family," reinforcement, and meaning, away from the farm.

The depth of the tentacles that delight in our collective rural delusion and the neglect that is real in rural America are deep. We have work to do. I have work to do. The state of "rural" is the underlying state of the nation and world. I would argue that everything with any value in life is dependent upon agriculture's health and revitalization or slow, painful death.

I now have a crystal clear perception of both radical edges of the ag spectrum and somewhere in the vast middle are many right answers.

I will begin with what I started learning more than a decade ago: we are sucking the resources that will save us dry ... human, plant, animal, water, soil, and air.

Of course, my few decades of awareness is minuscule compared to others with eyes wide open who have been focused on conservation for generations. Here I am now, though, compelled deeply every day that I have to do something. Yet, it so often feels daunting and like I am writing from the depth of a deaf wilderness.

What I absolutely know is the deprivation of our natural resources is and has been hands-down happening.

The soil is depleted nearly everywhere. Yet, there are also new practices to restore the soil and natural resources being implemented from sea to shining sea and across the world. However, we have acres upon acres to go.

My ink has run dry many times over writing about change that has been met with jeering, belligerence, hate, turned backs, and also (thank God) with gratitude, light bulb moments, and even a few miracles that I will firmly and forever believe in.

More truth … some aquifers are not facing dire lowering levels of water; however, they are facing serious water quality issues.

In many other areas across this very state, as well as the nation and world, wells have indeed run dry. I have leaned my hand on the skeletal remains of these pivots. I have watched the dust blow all around them. I have watched farmers fall to their knees desperately looking for a seed to sprout. It doesn't matter in those areas if winds blow those pivots over. They cannot use them … ever, again.

Some egos are too conditioned from having the privilege of water their entire lives, to see the blatant fact that while their aquifers may replenish right now, the world will be vying and is vying for their water. The mandates and laws will come. There are plans being made. I have heard those plans spoken about. The wars will come too if we don't wise up.

Let's talk about municipal water issues and nitrate levels so high schoolchildren are prohibited from drinking it.

And, do we think the war going on in schools has anything to do with our collective sucking dry of our natural resources? Has the gradual and strategic elimination of human beings from the agrarian landscape into struggling small towns, packed cities, reservations, juvenile detention centers, and prisons led to societal health?

You bet there is a correlation between violence, our medical crisis, and the loss of the agrarian foundation from our national ethos.

So, I have to admit, I am afraid. I absolutely am. I have had to choke down my fears with every single step I have made, every job change, and every word I write about the agriculture I still so deeply love.

But, it's an agriculture that has lost its most important resource … The CULTURE portion of the word. However, my fears have leveled out now and been replaced with the utmost confidence in what we can actually do for ourselves. If we indeed use our choices we still have, now. If we don't, shame on us. If we don't, I shudder to think what life will be like for our descendants.

When I began to learn there were people changing their farming practices because they were also afraid and ready to be on freedom's plan, I enthusiastically joined this disjointed effort with its fair share of problems and divisions too. But, despite their imperfections, these farming and ranching neighbors are vastly different. They are actually doing something about the serious issues facing agriculture and I continue to be inspired. The difference between these ag groups and others is their sense of purpose and self awareness. They look beyond their self interests to the betterment of the greater community while others are protectionists for their interests alone.

I began to travel and see the changes firsthand. I began to write about them. I was afforded chances I do not take for granted and I wanted to share the experiences with others at home just trying to keep farms and ranches going.

While doing so, I disenfranchised myself from some people in my little portion of the world. It's a small area here in irrigated corn country compared to the vastness of the earth and universe. But, I assure you, people worldwide are watching the careful or wasteful utilization of every inch of soil and drop of water we use. They are scratching their heads. Sometimes they are shocked by our wastefulness. Sometimes it brings them to tears. I have seen these tears. I have seen their disdain for the farmers and their families that I love. But I understand why now.

A friend from Africa asked me, "Have any of the farmers in your area carried their water for miles to irrigate crops and to literally survive? It appears not."

My writing began creating a cavernous abyss between myself and some members of my own family even. I mean, I was writing about my love for agriculture, but I was also writing about people doing something different. I learned I was a threat to all they had known and all they had been told. I was threatening their way of farming and way of life.

I discovered there are those secure in a system that rewards their way of life and others are literally fighting the same system to save their lives. These scenarios literally live next door to one another. Those scenarios were explicitly designed to separate us.

I had no idea the offense people would take to saying "no" to so many synthetic inputs (a long list that has now been proven to cause cancer and many other health issues). Why is saying yes to practices such as mob grazing cattle, growing cover crops, diversifying crops and livestock, planting more trees and perennials, protecting pollinators, and preserving water and soil resources so offensive to some? Can "progressive farming" evolve from pouring the coals to everything and pushing our natural resources to the limits, to instead a vision for agriculture where true stewardship in word and deed is most admired?

I also had no idea when advocating for the family farm I would be competing with the powerful propaganda of high-dollar advertising and marketing firms who are paid to promote the "corporation" is now the true champion of the "family farm."

I had no idea how divisive it would get. I do now.

Cooperation. Dedication. Hard work. Care. Concern. Community. Love. Life. Liberty. I still believe in these things. But some of the archaic ways we pursue trying to achieve those ideals are not leading to the outcomes we expected.

We are sucking precious resources dry. So many moms are tired. So many dads are worn out. Grandparents, wanting to help and make up for the time they lost with their own kids, are raising grandchildren. Many banks are stagnant and lack creativity in what they loan money for and what they don't because they have lost touch for a host of reasons. The government is clearly losing it, blinded by greed, imbalance, and inequality embedded in the foundation from the very start. Decisions are not being made. The blame game reigns supreme and "status quo" has no status anymore.

And here we all are standing in the status that is real life.

There is hope, neighbors. I absolutely know because I have seen the light from the gutter and I am walking a bit broken, but far more self-assured with an actual backbone, to the healing haven of the garden we can all share.

I have seen the light.

I have seen the lightbulb when a farmer, under the harsh thumb or even fist of dad or grandpa, radiantly goes on inside their minds and they decide for themselves and families what they are going to do.

So, maybe it's as simple as having faith and believing in ourselves and believing in the best in each other.

I know I believe …

I believe in the precious resource that is you, the U.S. and world's farmer and rancher.

I believe in the precious resource that is you the mom, dad, grandpa, grandma, aunt, uncle, son, daughter, neighbor, and friend.

I believe in the precious resource that is you, young professional, who is capable of taking the issue of our time head on with fortitude and grace and make something of it.

I believe in the precious resource that is you, city cousin we so desperately need insight and ideas from.

I believe in the precious resources that are still out here on farms and ranches making it, hanging on, thriving, and some literally dying just trying to hold on.

I believe in the family farms that have the most precious resources still growing up on them … our children, with dreams and new ideas of their own.

What is the meaning of life? The next generation all around gives life meaning. I believe in them. I believe in something better. I believe we can do something about it before it's too late.

So, my very able neighbors here and worldwide, what are we going to make better today? Because, we can or we won't. It's up to us.

She's the Wind, She's Nebraska

Kerry Hoffschneider | April 13, 2022
Seeds: Published on Tuesday, April 12 - York-News Times

I grew up surrounded by her beatings and blessings. If you're a Nebraskan, you know her – she's the Nebraska wind.

She whistles through creaking doors in the uneven hallways of old farmhouses.

She rips off shingles and pummels land to dust too quickly after rain.

She is that voiceless voice that can give little rest when she chooses to whip through our ears.

We grow used to her most days and fold hats around our heads or pull up hoods to block her boldness when we need to.

Nebraskans are not conditioned by silence. Oh no, they are conditioned by the wind.

These were and always will be windswept plains. Swept, long before we came swooping in.

What was meant to grow here were grasses with anchors many feet deep, that sway with backs naturally bowing down to the truth these old, wise plants simply know – bend or break, because there is no breaking her.

The more we push against the soil and wind, the more the soil and wind push back, or just go dormant and keep blowing away, waiting for the fight to be over to sprout the earth to life again. They both know we put up a fight we can't ultimately win. They know they will be here long after we're gone. They were chosen, (not us), to be first and last.

The Nebraska wind can explode into a tornadic rage and her lessons can shatter our futile attempts to contain her. She shreds our sheds and spits out homes and grain bins on her worst days, as if to say – "I've had enough. I was here first. Just try me."

But she wraps us in enough gentle warmth in the summer and serves up enough calm, autumn breezes for us to stay. We love her entirety too much to just leave her blusteriness behind. Because in Nebraska, a beautiful day is the most beautiful day ever. Those who nestle into her native prairie, hide away in her majestic Sandhills, and explore the art and color of her cities know – there's magic in Nebraska.

Let the Nebraska wind be your guide to the incredible adventures the land beneath embodies. She knows as she has touched every inch.

The grazing animal suits the Nebraska wind, like the bison that ran with her breath eons before we tried to domesticate a spirit that really cannot be tamed. Millenia spent in courtship, the bison and wind became one. They roamed under her direction with backs curved divinely and succinctly with whatever turn she took – north, south, east, and west.

Mightier than our ego and more innately wise, the Nebraska wind knows we have nothing to teach her. She drives every move beneath her expanse and determines what will, or will not, go on.

Heed her warning and enjoy her moments of peace. She's gracious enough to allow flowers to grow and families too. She doesn't dissolve every raindrop, nor does she whip us to death. But when she needs to, the lashings will be there. Then they will cease, and we can marvel at how wildly beautiful she is.

Yes, despite her worst days, her best days are always far better – that's why we stay under her direction. We have no choice but to go along. Ultimately, wherever she blows, we'll go.

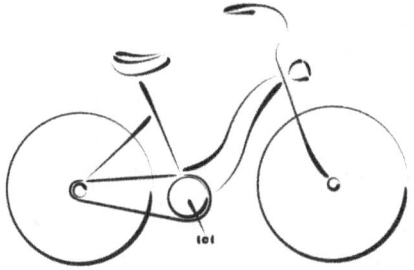

Farm Bike Tires

Kerry Hoffschneider | March 18, 2022
SEEDS column: published
Tuesday, March 15, 2022 - York News-Times

A brief moment of spring-like weather meant the bike came out on the farm recently just before old man winter decided he wasn't done with us quite yet. As Caroline dragged her bike to the air compressor, I considered the lasting impacts of the farm bike tire in many a farm kids' lives.

As the world turns, oftentimes farm bike tires struggle to make the rounds – it's a phenomenon really and not for the faint of heart, keeping these tires aired up.

Farm bikes and their accompanying tires have traveled miles upon miles by many-a-rider throughout history. Some of these bikes were passed down through generations. Others are shiny and new – gifts for eight-year-old birthdays or the 10-speed, an ideal way to celebrate entering the teen years. Regardless of the type of bike, the farm bike tires are where the rubber really meets the road. Even the shiniest models come to a screeching halt if these tires go flat – and oh boy, do they ever.

Yes, farm bike tires have tremendous hurdles. Nails being one. Ruthless stickers off plants that seem to mimic nails and target bike tires are another. There are countless barriers to farm bike tires staying blown up – yet these farm kids seem to find a way to ride on.

Farm bike tire riders also know these fragile tires are here for more altruistic reasons too. It's as if the universe around the farm is sending direct messages through these farm bike tires to adults scurrying around thinking they have to keep every nose-to-the grindstone task going.

Yes, these little tires are an oracle of wisdom releasing messages through the air as they slowly or speedily go flat – messages to farm dads, grandpas, and moms (when the two other options aren't available). It's as if they are calling out and saying, "Stop a minute. The next generation needs to get these wheels rolling. Whatever you are doing can wait!"

Yes, the world may not stop for much on the farm, but somehow everything comes to a halt when the farmer's daughter or son has a flat, farm bike tire. A world bound and determined to leave country roads behind means much has been lost from the family farm. It will be a sad day indeed when there's no more time for airing up farm bike tires.

Bike rides hold irreplaceable lessons like what it's like to traverse the plains in 110-degree heat or venturing out in wide open spaces with nothing more than a banana seat and big dreams. Without a farm bike, kids just wouldn't know the joys of pumping those pedals through thick gravel uphill and the wisdom that comes from knowing when you move over to the side of the road to allow vehicles to whiz by.

Awe yes, farm bike tires remind us we are mere mortals. As we hook up GPS and whatever we think is the latest and greatest on the ol' farm, these farm bike tires bring us to our knees. They are among the most humbling duties on a farm – they, along with raising farm kids in these far from simple times.

As frustrating as these tires can be, they ride through all sorts of weather. Even when tractors set idle on soggy, wet days, the farm bike tires find their way. Yes, rain or shine these tires get along fine. Their riders have a rare sort of endurance that comes from country roads. They know it's a rite of passage before the learning permit evolves these farm bike tires into real tires. So, for now, I'll hold onto the memories in the making while they hold onto those handlebars for a few more rides. Someday we will miss those farm bike tire memories and even long for the days we had to stop and air them up. God willing, another generation will come along and ask their grandparents to contend with those farm bike tires all over again and life will keep rolling along.

In the Heartland?

KERRY HOFFSCHNEIDER | AUGUST 24, 2021

A CORNFIELD IN THE HEARTLAND.

Growing up in the heartland I could not understand why some people could not see the pain of children.
Or the isolation of families.
Or the breaking of hearts.
In the heartland? Why?
They would even sometimes stoop to mocking what they pushed out or left out.
Reduced to gory gossip around tables some were welcomed around, and others were absolutely not.
Deplorable, yes.
Blinded by the calling of cornfields, yes, that too.
Too much, (even of a good thing), is often not a good thing.

Deep breath. I've said it. Write on . . .

We've driven away so much of what is genuine, precious, and valuable with our "abundance."

Somewhere a Native American mother desperately tries to hold it together for her family living in unnecessary poverty – descendants of humans criminally shoved aside.

Somewhere a grandmother remembers happier harvest days on the farm they lost in the 80s.

There's a son dying of alcoholism while his parents drive on by to church on Sunday.

There are families who just don't know what to do. You are not alone.

Is loneliness a symptom of modern agriculture? You bet it is.

These are also the subjects of agriculture.

Are they truths too large for our prairie pride?

It's the government they say.

It's my goddamned neighbor.

It's the bank that we deplore but are beholden to.

It's the favored son.

It's the black sheep.

It's the unruly wife.

It's so hard to share. But it's also . . .

A student getting raped at the frat party.

A son shooting up heroin to survive the stress of saving the family farm.

A child starving themselves to control their lives hoping they just fade away.

It's the high cost of everything we continue to willingly buy.

But really, what is it?

Should we stop and think?

Can we really think?

Or did the thinking leave when community was replaced by competition and what survived most are tasks and greed?

Or maybe it's because – we've always done it this way.

I grew up pondering all of this, peering out of a bedroom window in the upstairs of a farmhouse that seemed a thousand miles away from making sense.

I lived beautiful days and days more depraved than the business of back alleys.

I asked, why?

I still do.

I won't stop writing until healing and helping, not chasing yield, is truly the hope and bounty of the land.

Harsh words. I know.

I cringe when writing them.

But I think of the strength and sacrifice of the God who never left my side. Therefore, I am humbled and encouraged to fumble on.

I think of so many harsh lives suffered through because of these uncomfortable truths.

Making the comfortable, uncomfortable.

Oh well. I'm tired. It's time to share the weight.

"But Kerry," some say. "It's not all like this."

I know. But it has been like this for far too many.

The unimaginable has happened to the land's sons and daughters – impacting all creatures great and small.

The unimaginable is not going away for generations unless we speak of it.

Prayers in – action.

My Grandma would say, "Shame on you."

I know, Grandma, "Shame on me. Shame on us."

So, the least I can do is write on.

The least I can do is try and do something.

The least we can collectively do can be the most we have ever done.

I learn. It's my weapon of choice.

I have seen the conditions others live in because the system is broken.

Some would be surprised the conditions I got myself in.

It's all part of the journey. It's okay. Peace.

I feel the mistakes and triumphs of ancestors.

I believe in what is good about agriculture.

I do not believe in what is not.

We know better.

If we do not know better, we can explore the very apparent options and shed our belligerent lenses.

I am meeting a host of people who have stepped into the fray to fight for an agriculture that is free and boundless.

Because they know it's a fight for our lives.

They are fighting with seeds.

They are fighting with great sacrifice.

They are fighting to survive.

They are fighting fathers who don't agree with them.

They are fighting with themselves.

It's not too late.

Let's hearken the wisdom of the ages.

May the pride of agriculture be the fruitfulness of people, seeking the best for our neighbors.

May it be finding joy in healthy herds, grazing on healthy soils.

May it be growing nutrient dense, diverse crops.

May it be enjoying the natural world and the gifts of others displayed.

May it be enjoying being ourselves.

The sale barns and store fronts open.

The sidewalks full.

Communities alive.

Let's try something new.

I believe we can do better. Because we have done better in the past.

Some of us lost our way.

We can find our way back.

Or . . . we won't.

She's Nebraska

KERRY HOFFSCHNEIDER | APRIL 13, 2021
SEEDS WAS ORIGINALLY PUBLISHED
IN THE YORK NEWS-TIMES TUESDAY, AUG. 13

Nebraska doesn't typically whisper, instead she blows one season into the next.

That is her stature – withstanding it all.

She knows something we do not know.

She has endured winds we have not seen and will endure winds we will not see.

And she blows, and she blows – seasons come, seasons go.

On that rare, windless day, she allows us but a second in universe time to watch the green grass grow.

The ditches on walks are less lonely, no longer bare in brown.

How many cars have these ditches seen come and go?

Think of the prairie before there were roads – before time was recorded and yet still passed by.

Overseen by the sky, she's broad with waters deep and waters above.

Nebraska holds a sea of grass in one hand and cityscapes in the other.

She proudly bares the Western Meadowlark, Nebraska Goldenrod, the visiting Sandhill Cranes and the footprints, hoof prints and all the steps that have traversed upon her body.

Steadfast, she is part of the center holding the continent together – the precious glue of the country.

But she knows no country, just deeply knows herself, and that is her lesson for us – to know ourselves and enjoy her too.

I'd like to think the people who choose to reside upon her are the glue for the continent too. Maybe if we remember we are the center – we can strike that balance between extremes again.

But Nebraska has her extremes too – harsh, hearty, and delicate too. You just never know in Nebraska what the next day may bring.

She pushes through, with a few surprises along the way.

Yes, you can glow in a southern bouquet of flowers. But the grass making its way up through a gravel road in Nebraska stands out.

Climbing and reaching over rocks and through dark caverns, these thrill seekers of the plant world seek a stand-alone spot in Nebraska.

I would agree that you shouldn't doubt a flower that has sprung to life suckling only the dew from the side of a mountain rock.

And one should never, ever tread on a bloom standing tall in the desert.

But there is nothing like blades of grass growing from depths of experience on a Nebraska gravel road.

There really is no place like Nebraska and she prefers to be no place else either.

We are allowed to enjoy her blooming for a short, spring breath.

Then she'll be hot for a minute in her summer attire – and then she'll be gone.

So she goes.

So life goes.

She's Nebraska.

Don't do what Mother Nature will do for Free

KERRY HOFFSCHNEIDER | JANUARY 8, 2024

MONROE, Neb. – John and Susan Nelson say they aren't unlike other farmers, they want to leave the farm better than they got it. But, in order to do so, they said they needed to start learning some new ideas. Today the Nelsons grow corn, organic blue corn, and soybeans on their Nebraska farm. In Kansas, they farm wheat, corn, and milo. They have also instituted some cover crops that help retain the moisture in the soil and enhance microbial activity.

"During the drought, I was riding with a neighbor in the combine near our Decatur County, Kansas farm. They had moved a fence line on a pasture to farm the area. The new farm ground was located on native pasture ground. The corn they grew on that native pastureland looked like an irrigated field, and the rest of the farm was hardly worth harvesting. I really started to think, 'Man has done something to make this land worse.' I asked myself, 'What can we do to get the land recovered and turn it back to what it once was?'"

The Nelsons farm with their son, Andrew, who has a diesel technology degree and also runs a repair shop. Their daughter, Courtney, has a degree in mechanized systems management and is passionate about ag education. They also farm with John's brother Darren and his wife Stacy, and work and learn from a network of people including John Hannah and Brad Uehlin. Hannah is a Nebraska crop consultant and active member of the Lower Platte North Natural Resources District (NRD) board. Uehlin is a friend from Kansas who has flown cover crops on for them and enjoys trying new things.

Susan grew up in Belgrade, Neb. on a farm and embraced the rural life as a wife and mother. "When I got married, I stayed home with the kids and helped John full time. I can run most of the equipment, and I also do all the paperwork. When it comes to making changes on the farm like cover crops, we have started out slow on a few of our farms. We didn't see a major difference in the first couple of years with cover crops. That's when people usually quit, right before they start seeing the benefits. But now, we are seeing the positives."

"The kids were always with us growing up on the farm; they would ride with us no matter what we were doing," Susan went on about both their children's formative years growing up in the country. "The more we did, the more I helped with operations such as cultivating, driving the semi, running the combine, whatever was needed. Even when we started farming in Kansas, during harvest, the kids would go with us."

"We're very proud of the kids," Susan said. "They work hard."

John has always lived the farm life, too. "I grew up farming just five miles to the northwest of our current home and started farming when I was a kid. We baled hay, had some cattle, and raised hogs too when I was in high school. In 1992 when I married Susan, we were still raising hogs and then we all know the hog market crashed in the mid-90s."

While the Nelsons did get out of the hog business, they continued to recognize the value of livestock in agriculture. The couple runs their neighbor's cattle on the land. John said the cattle are beneficial for the manure and, "The cattle also break up the stalks. We want those stalks returning to the earth for the soil microbial activity."

Cover crops also greatly help enhance soil microbial activity and water infiltration as well, John said. "In the first couple of years trying our rye cover crops, Susan is right, we did not see a lot of benefits. Then I was listening to one of Gabe Brown's presentations when he said you may not see benefits until the third or fourth year. He was right. We are seeing the water infiltration improve greatly and that is just one of the benefits we are seeing."

"We also started applying manure again instead of commercial phosphates, because we weren't getting the response from it," John noted. "And, we stopped tilling altogether and went to strip-till. Early on, we went through a spell where we could count up to four years of trash in the field, including the bean stubble. Now our trash is deteriorating rapidly in the months of July and August because of the microbial activity we have going on in the soil. I don't work the manure into the ground. I plant rye when spreading the manure and get the benefits of the cover crop and the natural fertilizer. I am also finding some of the best results if I drill the rye into soybean stubble and we are trying to fly some of the rye onto corn stalks, too, and finding some success."

"Probably the best showcase of cover crop success for us was in Kansas where we were trying oats. Where we planted the oats before wheat, the ground is the most mellow," he went on. "We compared two different fields when we had a three-inch rain at the end of August and another two-and-a-half-inch rain ten days after that. We noticed all the water soaked into the ground where we planted the oats, and the terraces were not filled with water either."

"One thing we would like to figure out is how to use a drone to plant cover crops ahead of the wheat harvest," he added.

"Courtney has her drone license," Susan explained. "It's just a matter of finding the time to do it and weighing the cost of purchasing a drone with the other costs on the farm."

Farmers and ranchers weighing costs is nothing new under the sun. John said, "With the challenge of machinery prices, tight margins, and all the other costs, it's rewarding to see the results we are trying with new practices that benefit the soil."

"We want to keep farming because it's what we know and what we've always done," Susan added. "With farming comes continual improvement and innovation."

John reiterated time and again, "Don't do what Mother Nature will do for free."

Spanish Teacher, Market Gardener, and Mexico Traveler

Kerry Hoffschneider | December 29, 2023

When she's not teaching students Spanish at Centennial Public Schools, you can find Emily Petersen making her way around the acreage of her dreams just outside Seward, Neb.

"The other day I was walking around outside with my overalls and thinking to myself, 'I am just a little old man farmer out here,'" Petersen said laughing.

Petersen has a farmer's heart indeed, surrounded by ducks, goats, chickens, farm cats, and her beloved dog, she spends the winter dreaming of her summer gardens and farmer's markets where she sells everything from pumpkins to gourds, tomatoes, peppers, squash, and lots of green beans.

"One day I picked 17 pounds of green beans. That was a big day," she admitted, laughing about how glad she is that day is over. "But I'll probably try and grow that many again!"

"I like repurposing stuff," the self-proclaimed "little old farmer" (who is actually a young, vibrant schoolteacher) said about the self-sufficient farm she is building. "The goats are my garbage disposals. The chickens eat scraps, too. The hay out in the pasture goes to feed my animals and I can use their manure to fertilize the gardens."

Petersen learned some of her industrious, hardworking skills growing up the daughter of Stu and Lynette Petersen. Stu co-owns Utica Parts & Service and Lynette is a teacher at Seward High School. "My parents have been so helpful. They helped me turn the granary into a chicken coop and helped with so many things around here, too many to name. They are super hard workers and such good people. I am very lucky."

Her parents have been very supportive of their daughter's adventurous, can-do spirit in many ways throughout her formative years and into college as well. "I went to Seward High School and then the University of Nebraska-Kearney (UNK), intending on being a veterinarian. I loved animals my entire life. The chemistry and biology were really hard though, and I thought that was a sign I needed to change my major to Spanish."

"I had taken all the Spanish classes UNK offered, but needed a few more credits. That's when the opportunity to study abroad came around. UNK had a connection with the Universidad De Quintana Roo in Southern Mexico. We had a student at UNK from there in an exchange program, but no one from the college had ever traveled there. So, I decided to go," she explained.

"I was honestly terrified and figured I would back out in the end, but then it got to the day I was leaving, and I was like, 'Okay, this is really happening.' My parents took me to the airport, and I was flying blind.

On the plane I cried, 'What if my friends forget about me? What if I don't make any friends?' I definitely had fears about missing what was going on in Nebraska and told my friends and family, 'You can't have fun without me. You can't forget about me when I am gone.' But then it turned out to be the best thing I have ever done," she admitted.

"When I arrived in Mexico, I had one lady who had been contacting me from the university who picked me up from the airport and set me up with a room for the night. The next day we went apartment hunting. We toured some apartments and found one pretty close to campus. It was definitely different than I had envisioned. There were no screens on the windows and no air conditioning. The apartment had a bed, bed sheets, and an armchair. I didn't need a lot of covers because it was so hot. It also had a kitchen table and microwave, but no television. I didn't even miss the television," she said.

"I did not have a refrigerator, so everything was purchased pretty much fresh. I would buy baguette bread and tortillas and sometimes go to a restaurant. I did miss the ice water," Petersen admitted.

Life in Mexico became more exciting when Petersen began making friends. One of them was a very close friend named Arturo who showed her the ropes. "There were only four apartments in my building and his apartment was catty-corner from mine. We became fast friends and helped each other a lot. He was trying to learn English and I was of course trying to strengthen my Spanish. I would be walking around looking for places to get food and then as I got to know him, he said we should go to the grocery store together. He'd say, 'Let's grab a cab and go.' He knew the area far better and that made it enjoyable."

"We ate a lot of scrambled eggs with chorizo sausage there," she went on. "I still crave that, but it doesn't taste as good here as it did there. It's just not the same. Everything was so fresh there, too. Lots of fresh peppers and avocado would just fall off the trees. There were lots of fresh fruits like pineapple, too, and rambutan, a fruit that looks sort of like a strawberry with spindly-type deals all over them."

"Overall, I felt very safe in the quiet neighborhood in the town of Chetumal," she noted adamantly.

A month into her nearly five-month stay, Petersen's parents came to visit and to learn. "My parents were nervous, but I think their visit calmed many of their fears. It was great to have them."

While at the Universidad, Petersen took a Spanish for Foreigners class, a French class, and a Biodiversity course. "I learned how everyday people speak instead of just out of a textbook. Some of the things I had learned in high school and college were Spain-based teachings and I was in Central America, so the words were different than what I had learned before. I also learned to get over the fact that I was worried about offending people there with my language acumen. I made a bit of a fool of myself sometimes, but everyone was always kind to me about it."

"It was hard to leave because I knew I may never get to come back and it was just a great experience," Petersen said looking back.

Back home, Petersen started working at a seed company, still not knowing she was going to be a Spanish teacher. Then her mom encouraged her to job shadow a Spanish teacher and, she said, "Sitting in that classroom I was like, 'Yes! This is what I want to do.'"

Petersen headed to Doane University to complete a fast-track program they have for people who want to be teachers. She graduated in December of 2009. "I taught at Cross County for three years and then it actually worked out perfectly because I had bought a house in Utica and then Centennial had a job opening. I started as a teacher at Centennial in August of 2015."

She often reflects on the cultural attributes of the life she loved in Mexico – the fresh vegetables that she is now raising here, taking time to visit more, intergenerational family closeness. "We don't always have to be so busy running here and there. We need to slow down and be humans more instead of being so scheduled to death all the time. Life in Mexico taught me that."

Petersen said at least once a year she tells her Spanish students about her experiences south of the border. "It helps me as a teacher. I hope students will remember my stories and consider traveling there. You can spend half the money and see just as beautiful beaches in Mexico as nearly anywhere else. Yes, there are dangers to look out for like anywhere in the United States, you just have to be wise and seek out good travel advice."

"There are good people in every corner of the planet," Petersen said. "My experiences in Mexico showed me that."

The little "old, young farmer" and Spanish teacher in Seward County is one of those good people. We're lucky to have her experiences making a difference back in Nebraska.

The Great Mauck Relay Cropping Reset

Kerry Hoffschneider | December 21, 2023

Jason Mauck speaking at Acres USA.

The Graze Master Group wanted Jason Mauck as a partner because he's willing to change, learn, and dream. It's going to be very exciting to cover what he is doing in the months and years ahead. We're proud of him. Here's an introduction to this "Fibonacci Farmer," taking relay-cropping to the next level.

He's calling it, "The Great Mauck Reset," at Mauck Farms in Gaston, Ind. Mauck is changing things that he can with gusto and trying a different approach to farming through relay cropping wheat, soybeans, and corn with what he calls "God's math" – the Golden Ratio. A "golden rule" of farming based on the fascinating science of the Fibonacci code that is expressed in his genuine love for growing more abundance in tune with the sun, soil, water, and all of life.

The circumstances in Mauck's life that led to him farming in new ways are rooted in challenging farm economics coupled with abrupt and unexpected pain and loss. Early on in his career, life was unfolding well at Mauck Farms where Jason's dad Bill and grandpa James were keeping things going while he was building a landscaping business of his own.

"What really changed my life was when corn went to $1.80, and beans were also cheap. My parents, Bev and Bill, said get a job and make some money. That is when I began building my landscaping business where I learned how to relay crop," he explained.

"It was completely a practical deal," he went on. "I am inherently cheap, and I really like being resourceful. So instead of marketing the landscaping business through different types of advertising, it was more effective to create living billboards around commercial properties and homes. I took a lot of pride in my floral arrangements and started relay cropping summer flowers into bulbs and pansies. I would have like five or ten dollars into the floral displays. I would let them grow together and pluck out the spring stuff and kept the flowers that I could keep as bulbs. It just became practical."

The relay cropping landscape math worked out in his favor. For example, he said, "An old daylily in a landscape bed could be sliced into eight plants pretty easily, bigger than the ones for $15 each at the supply store."

"The landscape business was going well and then my dad got pancreatic cancer. We found out in the fall and by April he was gone. He was 53. That's when I stepped into his shoes on the farm," he said. "Then my uncle Lewis died at 54, nearly the same age as my dad. I lost the drive to farm more, and more, and more, and started looking at what we could actually do differently with what we already have."

Today, Mauck's mindset change is one of the most valuable resources being applied on the farm. "When dad died, that put an end to the industrial ag way of thinking in my mind. I was more comfortable with a canopy of plants and the relay cropping approach to farming that I was implementing in my landscape business. Instead of the 'scorched earth' industrial methods, I wanted to pursue an approach more in-tune with nature."

Every day, Mauck is tirelessly striving to take a deep look and assessment of how well he is using the economic resources from the industrialized farming methods his grandfather and father successfully implemented. Instead of dwelling on everything the industrialized system may have done wrong, he is utilizing some of the assets to find more harmony and balance with nature in a highly profitable way through relay cropping.

"My first conventional crop year was 2011 after dad's death. It just kept raining and raining," he recalled. "I planted stuff in the mud, and it rained more. I poured everything into the work ethic. Pain teaches. Adversity creates adaptations in nature. Striving is living. I also knew when you change, you're not going to change anyone else's mind until you prove things. You have to make the commitment to learn and share what you are learning. That's when I also started to talk to new people and learn from them, too."

Mauck now helps work around 3,000 acres of corn, soybeans, and wheat in addition to finishing 25,000 hogs in a calendar year. For nine years, he has also been relay cropping 300 acres of soybeans, wheat, and corn. This relay cropping is inspired by the Fibonacci code he explained. "Our bodies, plants, anything under the sun follows a specific pattern. That pattern, in numerical terms, is the Fibonacci Sequence, a sequence where each number is the sum of the two preceding ones. Fibonacci numbers have a ratio very close to the Golden Ratio that is approximately 1.618."

If one takes a walk with Mauck long enough, he will point out the manifestation of the Fibonacci code in shapes all over the place, especially in the curves in his relay-cropped fields where you will find him, his sons – Case and Liam – wife Kortnee, friends, family, and the dogs immersed in the miracle of it all. This ratio appears all over the place, he noted – from art, to facial features, to architecture, and everywhere in nature.

"The goal is to empower the genetic expression found in nature and mitigate the risk of both too much rainfall and too little," he said about the "magic" that occurs when growing crops in tandem with each other. "In other words, it's asking ourselves, 'How can we design a harmonious relationship between a cereal and a summer annual?'"

"We actually aren't planting half of the field in wheat. We're planting 1:1.618 (the Golden Ratio)," he explained. "In order to grow nearly the same soybean yields as we would if planting alone, we must space the wheat at 1:1.618 and change the seeding rate. This allows the direct sunlight down through the crop canopy so the beans can flourish while the wheat is growing in an amplified avenue as well."

The relay cropping scenario allows Mauck to harvest the cereal that dies a natural death, "instead of terminating the cereal grain with glyphosate, lowering the revenue per acre, adding to costs, and not getting the full benefit of the cereal. Also, the soybean yields may even be greater than beans growing alone (not in a relay cropping scenario) in the wetter springs which have been more prevalent than dry ones. If it's dry, the beans are slightly shaded, and the wheat will yield better with more abundant sunshine. The 'trash' when harvesting the wheat acts as a mulch and preserves moisture."

The Golden Ratio is benefiting the pocketbook, and turning into real profits too. "The reason I can get up to $1,500/acre in revenue in some cases on less than $200 in true input costs (like seed, chemical, and manure) is because I am hacking into exponentials on the farm. Exponentials can be tough to explain to some people because they want specific instructions, and it takes a few years of learning your own circumstances and context on your farm to know what works best for you."

"I spent years trying to grow 300-bushel corn. I saw the yield potential of our crops, but I also saw the unintended consequences of pushing crops, both in spending money that wasn't needed and the issue of things that don't work out exactly as I wished. I would add nitrogen multiple times of year and fungicide and get aphids because the crop had too much nitrogen and I was killing the beneficial insects," he explained, noting he could talk hours about the savings and benefits he is seeing.

Mauck admits there's no doubt his can-do personality is something he learned from his mom, dad, and grandpa. He also greatly appreciates his uncles, Mike and David Mauck, and his cousin Neil for their hard work, vital roles, and dedication to Mauck Farms as well. Mauck, a people person, said there are simply too many friends and family that mean the world to him to list them all in the story.

His can-do spirit is being noticed beyond his backyard, too. *Successful Farming* named Mauck on its "10 Up and Comers in Agriculture" list in 2017 for his leadership and collaborative efforts. Since then, he has also spoken at numerous events about the money he is saving and the increase in bounty he is producing on the farm through these relay cropping methods.

But it's really not about him at all. Mauck really wanted to reiterate that "I can teach my kids how to push a button in ten seconds on a tractor. What I really want them to have is a deeper understanding of what's really going on in the soil, what really matters about life on the farm, you know? What gets me up in the morning is trying to make positive changes. We are losing our intergenerational knowledge. We're losing our liberties and freedoms."

Kortnee, an English teacher, coined a hashtag #farmweird to explain her husband's experiments with new methods. "She knows I just love this kind of stuff and maybe this is weird in the grand scheme of things, but for me it's about being harmonious with nature. It's all about managing life with life with arrangements that can create dynamic venues that mitigate risks and empower each seed and sun ray. Together we can learn ways to produce more with less."

Mauck's grandpa is in the nursing home now, but there are still plenty of discussions between the two men. They don't always agree, and he respects that. One way he made inroads with grandpa's skepticism was buying a combine of his own.

"My combine. My rules," he said grinning about the many ways he has tried to prove himself to the man he deeply respects and that helped shape his independence.

"I want to strengthen resiliency in my soil and build resiliency in my relationships," Mauck said adamantly. "I am very confident farming in this way works and I love it. It comes down to striving to help people, building community, and trying to do what is right."

"My Grandpa Mauck said, 'Take care of the land, it'll take care of you.'"

Mauck is doing just that by changing things up a bit to honor his father and grandpa and to ensure the farm's resources are fruitful for generations to come.

There's no way to capture everything Mauck is doing to change. That is why we're not done writing about his vision. Stay tuned for more stories from Mauck Farms and how he is working with his friend Zack Smith, the visionary behind the Stock Cropper, in their quest to make farming autonomous and exponentially regenerative with multiple livestock species grazing across the field in a really cool, solar-powered piece of equipment. The #farmweird fun never ends!

Make sure to follow Mauck at: www.facebook.com/jason.mauck.5 and on X @jasonmauck1

A Better Way to Farm

KERRY HOFFSCHNEIDER | NOVEMBER 2, 2023

Last year, Allen Hensley was talking to his friend Ryan Harlan who told him, "There has to be a better way to farm."

The two Texas farmers were talking about farming more efficiently and profitably, with less disturbance of the soil, fewer costly synthetic inputs, and less reliance on high-dollar machinery.

"I met Ryan with his dad. We were talking about seed," Hensley, a Rob-See-Co and Streamline Ag representative said. "Ryan is very meticulous when it comes to farming. He likes to come up with a plan and analyze things from a different angle. He will run a scenario by me, and I will present the 'what ifs.' We really became good friends because of that."

Trust, sharing new ideas, and presenting opportunities is at the core of their friendship and that is why Hensley immediately thought of Harlan when he learned about the Agoro Carbon program from Del Ficke, co-founder of the Graze Master Group. "Ryan seemed like he really fit the bill for the type of farmers the program applies to. He has an innovative mind and is always searching for the next thing to improve farming in his area and is just overall forward-thinking."

"When I talked to him a year ago, Ryan was starting to move away from conventional tillage and we started talking about different scenarios that include more cover crops and less synthetic inputs," Hensley explained.

"I was also learning more about the Graze Master Group from Del Ficke and Agoro Carbon is one of their many diverse partners," Hensley went on. "The more Del filled me in about Agoro Carbon, I knew it was a natural fit for Ryan."

Agoro Carbon Alliance offers farmers and ranchers a network of partners to help in the transition of their operation to more conservation practices. The company offers access to the carbon marketplace and income through quality verified carbon credits, provides long-term benefits to production, and minimizes risk.

"I told Ryan the Agoro Carbon program is a no-brainer for a farmer just starting to change. It's common sense. You can bring in Agoro Carbon and the Graze Master Group and you have a support network right there as you change directions and improve the health of your farm," Hensley reiterated.

Ryan Harlan's Farming Story – Nueces County Texas

"I am definitely turning heads," Harlan said about the 9,000 acres under his management that he has earned since farming as a child with his dad Steve and grandpa Jack. "I grew up in Bishop, Texas in a little town of 3,000 people or so. We grew up in town, but we'd go out to the farm and work all the time. It's the only job I have ever known, working on a farm. Today, my wife Robyn and I and our two kids – Bodie and Hattie – are the fifth generation on the farm."

"I have always enjoyed it and it has always been what I have wanted to do. It's very rewarding planting a seed and watching it grow," Harlan said with the heart of a farmer.

After graduating from high school, Harlan headed to the University of Texas in Austin where he earned his bachelor's in business management. "My parents (Steve and Shana) both said the farming can be here for you, but you need to go off and get some education and experience. That's why I chose a degree that is fairly universal. They were correct in giving me that advice."

Farming always pulled on his heart, though, and Harlan was soon back home helping out after college. He eventually met a beautiful lady named Robyn at his cousin's shower. Harlan would stop and see his future bride on the way to visit the family ranch land near Jourdanton, Texas. The couple was married on May 11, 2013, with a baby on the way two years later.

Back in 2011, after Harlan had just met Robyn, he was looking for a house to buy and came across a piece of land. "I told my stepdad John Prukop and mom about it. My stepdad said, 'Buy the land, but don't buy the house.' I told him I didn't have the down payment. He said just farm it and I will give you half the down payment and you pay me back when you can. So, I bought the land instead of the house and my mom and stepdad leased me 460 acres on top of the 160-acre farm I had also bought. He gave me great advice saying I needed to do that so I could get a loan and build farming history up with the bank so when it came to buy my father and grandfather out I could do it."

"I was trying to do what I could to be a better farmer," Harlan said about balancing farming his own 620 acres along with working full time for Harlan Farms. "I just kept getting a little more land on my own and in 2021, I was farming 2,400 acres on the side and still helping manage Harlan Farms that was around 6,800 acres at the time. My time was spread very thin."

"All that was taking place and then dad and grandpa said, 'We're ready to sell out.' Because of my stepdad's advice, I had a 10-year relationship with the bank, and I went to them, and they said, 'Yes, let's do it.'"

Today Harlan is farming just over 9,000 acres all in Nueces County with the help of his trusted team that he said he can't live without. "Robyn is the backbone of the family. We have six employees that work with us on the farm. My cousin Andrew Harlan works with me and Alberto Castro, who has been working with the Harlan family for 45 years. Those are two people I really rely on with decision making, and just talking about different scenarios. I put a lot of trust in them. Everyone working with us is so very important."

Harlan's farming goals are to be about a one-third split between corn, milo, and cotton. "Those are the resilient crops in our area. I have cut back my cotton acres compared to a lot of guys around here. A lot of that had to do with the dry planting season and getting the cotton out of the ground. The input costs are through the roof too, from planting the seed to taking care of it to harvesting and having to worry about a hurricane or heavy rains."

The average rainfall in his area is around 25 inches. "It's the hottest in August and early September. It can get upwards of 105 degrees with high humidity. It's just miserable. You can cut the air with a knife. Our coldest time is January to February, but we don't catch a really hard freeze except for maybe every eight to 10 years. That makes the weeds very hard to keep under control, but it also means we have a long growing season with a lot of opportunities."

Seeking new opportunities and ideas is why Harlan met Hensley. "Dad and I were looking for some different hybrids that were honestly a little cheaper that would work in our area. Allen had just started selling Rob-See-Co and he pointed us to some tough hybrids that worked in dry climates. We relied on his expertise as far as what to plant and where to plant. He really helped us a lot that first year, and every year since then. He has become one of my best friends, and a big reason is because we think so much alike."

With progressive and open minds, Harlan and Hensley were talking about farming differently all the time. "I was constantly asking myself, 'How can I be more sustainable and leave farming better than when I came into it?' I knew if we kept farming the conventional way, we weren't going to be productive in maybe 50 years or less. The climate is changing, and we really need to understand how to adjust for more extremes in temperature and rainfall. The way we've been able to make crops grow the last seven years is relying on the majority of our rainfall in one or two big rains. You catch that five or six-inch rain and you need to be very ready because it's going to get very dry again."

Readiness also comes in the form of figuring out the tillage and cover crop program that works. "All signs point to minimum till, no-till, and incorporating cover crops as the future of farming. It comes down to how you can make it work in our area because farmers have tried and failed. It's figuring out when to plant cover crops, when to shut them off, and how you work in a cover crop that fits your rainfall."

"We're also trying to find out which legumes work, and which warm season grasses will work," he went on. "It has been very quick learning. And, with all the cotton planted around here there is (chemical) drift from all the spraying. So, we're still searching for the right cover crop mix, and it may be one that works behind milo, one behind corn, and yet another one behind cotton."

This is why he said Agoro Carbon has made so much sense the first year the Harlan family is transitioning some of their acres to new practices. "Allen brought up Agoro Carbon to me. I had heard about carbon capture companies, but the older farmers would say, 'We can't capture carbon, we have to make the field black and loose and then smooth it out.' I had done that style of farming for many years too, but I wanted to change. So, I made the switch this year."

"If you're going to be moving that direction anyway, look at Agoro Carbon because they can help you implement some of the changes and there is up front money to help pay for things like minimum tillage and planting cover crops. Because farmers can capture the carbon that way. You can do however much or little you want. I was heading that direction anyway so partnering with Agoro Carbon and Graze Master was a no-brainer," he said adamantly.

One year in, Harlan is seeing changes. "We ended up doing 1,000 acres because I needed those broad acres to see if the peas I planted were going to work. One of the biggest benefits is leaving your soil structure in place and the water retention you start noticing. There is also a great increase in the number of birds, like Mourning doves."

"When I started farming, I always told myself I just wanted to be successful," he said, looking back. "That term is different for different people. I used to set yield goals, but that is hard in dryland farming. Then, when I started slowly thinking about minimum till and no-till farming, my mind shifted from successful to also sustainable."

"The goal for me now is being successful with what I am doing even if it's different than everyone else around me. By doing that, I am helping my soil profile handle the extremes between wet and dry. If I build the soil now, if Bodie and Hattie want to take over the farm one day, it's set up for them. Robyn is always encouraging me too and saying, 'If that is what you think we need to do, do it.' It's good to have the support of a few people in my family and friends like Allen Hensley because I am doing things differently out here. That's okay though, because it fuels me if people tell me that it's not going to work."

We Would be Lost Without Him

KERRY HOFFSCHNEIDER | OCTOBER 23, 2023

KEARNEY, Neb. – JaeRam Lee knows very clearly what it feels like to be lost in a foreign land. Lost, and then, found. The immigrant from South Korea has experienced the challenges and opportunities that one must undertake to be a permanent resident of the United States.

"My parents, KwangHee (father) and KyeongRan (mother), encouraged me very much to come to this country. I did not like the idea of coming here. I had family and friends back home in South Korea. I can say now that although I felt forced by my parents to come here by myself when I was 17, it has been a very good thing," Lee said about his journey to the U.S. that began in 2005.

Lee is currently serving as the Research and Development Technical Supervisor for Ward Laboratories, Inc. based out of Kearney, Neb. Nikki Kuhr, Lab Manager said, "We would be lost without him." The Ward Laboratories extended family of employees agree with Kuhr's sentiments.

The story of how Lee arrived at his professional career is a remarkable one. "I spent a year in Orange County, California as a foreign exchange student at Tustin High School and I was fortunate enough to have a really good host family. Not only did I learn a lot of English skills, but I also was able to travel to the majority of the National Parks in the U.S. during this time because they owned a really nice motor home and loved to travel."

"I really enjoyed the experience as an exchange student. I wanted to not only stay longer in the United States, but also wanted to study more and possibly graduate from a U.S. high school. But I wasn't able to attend public school as a foreigner. So, I had to find private schools in order to attend and finish high school in the U.S. We started looking for private schools that offered room and board and we contacted an agency specializing in studying abroad. They gave us three options and it came down to one school – Nebraska Christian Schools in Central City," he explained.

"I graduated and then thought to myself, 'Now what? Do I go back home or apply for college in the states?'" He said, looking back, "I applied to several schools and the University of Nebraska–Lincoln offered a scholarship. I was also eligible for in-state tuition because I had graduated from a high school in Nebraska."

When Lee was a sophomore in college, he had to return to South Korea because they have a mandatory military service requirement. "I was a helicopter mechanic and did that for two-and-a-half years and then came back and finished college with a degree in biochemistry and minors in math and chemistry."

In order to legally stay in the U.S., Lee needed to maintain his Visa status. When college ended, his status as a student would end as well. At this point, he needed to extend his Visa at graduate school or change to a work permit status.

"Back in college, I originally wanted to be a dentist. I had my pre-dentistry requisites done and then during my senior year it became overwhelming," he admitted.

Lee grappled with going on for another four years of schooling, residency, and internships. "I started to doubt myself and was not sure I wanted to invest more time and money in that unforeseen future."

This is when Lee applied for an OPT (Optional Practical Training) Program that allows foreign students who graduate from college a year of experience working in the U.S. Once in the program, Lee had 90 days to find a job. "If I didn't, I would be sent back home."

Lee was prepared to work diligently to find a job, but there was also the challenge of finding a place to live. His college housing was done, and it was difficult to find a rental contract for less than a year. "That's when I contacted a high school friend who lives near Aurora, Neb. and asked if I could crash at his place and help him farm. The Hunefeld family accepted me as their family member and went through the best and worst times of my life with me and supported me unconditionally. They are organic farmers, and I also learned a lot about the farm with them too."

Lee spent three months with the Hunefeld's. "I was in an area, though, where my job options were limited. I applied to several places in the surrounding area and then was lucky enough to get two interviews."

One of those interviews led to a position at a veterinary pharmaceutical company in Grand Island, Neb.. "I was very happy. Now I had one year for sure to work in the U.S. instead of having to go home. I was a quality control technician for the business."

Work life was positive, and Lee was thoroughly enjoying the opportunities that were opening up for him. Still, there was always a cloud of anticipation over him because his work Visa was going to expire in a year. "I was hesitant. I thought maybe I should go back to school or go back home. But I found the courage to ask my employer if there was any way they might be willing to sponsor my work Visa."

The business sponsored a two-year extension on the work Visa and even extended it another three years after that. "I always wondered how long I would be able to stay in the U.S., though. That is when I asked them if they could help sponsor my permanent residency. Instead of renewing the work Visa every year, that meant the employer is helping the employee stay. They are ultimately saying, 'This employee is a good asset to the company and is a good enough, and a skillful enough worker that we will put our company name behind him to sponsor him.'"

"Ultimately I wanted to stay in the states without having to renew my status every other year and even renewing wasn't guaranteed granted," he explained. "I was always in fear of the unforeseen future and the 'what if' scenario I was living in."

Lee said you can get permanent residency with sponsorship from an employer, and it used to be you also could if you joined the U.S. Army (but that has since changed). "You can also get it by marrying a U.S. citizen. Not only was I mentally and financially unprepared to get married, I also didn't think it was fair to bring someone into my life, buy a home, and start a family to have them go through the same thing I was going through with the unknowns in the future. Finding someone to marry at that point was not an option for me and it was probably going to be really hard to find someone who would like to be with me given my circumstances, anyways."

His employer started going through the process of helping Lee with the permanent residency; however, it was far more difficult than they thought and, "From a business standpoint, they made the difficult decision to not continue the process. I was very disappointed. But I understand they did what they thought was best for their business."

The taxpaying, hardworking, responsible employee continued to work for the company and once again the storm clouds gathered in his mind. "'Now what?' became something I asked myself often. I was feeling very depressed and extreme anxiety and pressure. I had about six months left at that point on my Visa. My co-workers, who had no power to help, were so bummed out and told me they couldn't believe what was happening. That support meant more than anything."

"I didn't lose hope," he went on. "I thought, just maybe someone else would hire me. With six months left, I knew I didn't have many options. Everywhere I applied online had it written in fine print, 'Do you require a Visa sponsorship?' That was hard because I knew they were sorting me out before I even got a chance to be interviewed."

With a month left on the Visa, reality was hitting fast. "Who else was going to take me on? Time was ticking along, and, in my head, I began to feel this anger and betrayal. I wanted to be a professional and do what was right." Facing the hard fact that he may have to sell everything and move back to South Korea, Lee started looking for jobs back in his homeland. "It was COVID during that time so online interviewing was a thing. I applied at a couple prestigious pharmaceutical companies in South Korea and my six years of working in the U.S. did pay off and I was able to get several interviews."

Lee relayed that South Korea is a very small country and jobs are very competitive to come by. "I had an interview and then a second interview with a lab manager there and after that the president, vice-president, and executives of the company interviewed me. This was all very eye-opening because the typical U.S. hiring process was not this way as much. I even had to be on an A.I. (artificial intelligence) monitored webcam so they could detect my emotions while I was taking tests. I was like, 'I get you are trying to find the best people, but like really? Is this what the world has come to?'"

The fear of being jobless, a failure, and the unknown began to weigh heavily on Lee. "Then I got an unexpected text message from Jordan Westengaard, (quality assurance and control manager at Ward Laboratories). Jordan had been my supervisor at the first veterinary pharmaceutical company. He randomly asked me to go to lunch. He actually felt a bit guilty because he was looking to hire me away from the other company. He had no idea I was going to be done there and was looking for a new opportunity."

Lee started telling Westengaard the story on a Friday and on Saturday, after speaking to Ryan Dennhardt – the human resources/business manager for Ward Laboratories – Westengaard said they thought they had a place for him. "I just didn't see how they could sponsor my permanent residency in less than a month. I was willing to go to work the next day if I had to, but I didn't believe it at first. I couldn't believe it after all I had been through. I was scared of starting over again and getting let down again. I had a lot of doubts since the company where I worked loyally for six years didn't want to sponsor me, then who would? Especially when I hadn't shown Ward Laboratories anything or proven anything yet. Everything was hard to believe and too good to be true."

"But I also thought, 'Maybe this is God's calling.' I didn't give up hope," he added confidently.

Lee contacted his immigration lawyer and told him he had a potential business to sponsor his permanent residency. "I asked him if this was even possible in a month's time. He told me there was no way in that short amount of time. He gave me the option of going back home and starting the process all over."

Soon after he was hired by Ward Laboratories, the time left on Lee's Visa expired. Lee was no longer able to work legally in the U.S. However, Ward laboratories kept their promise and worked with him on the process and waited patiently, "I got a loan to pay for my rent and worked until my permanent residency papers were completed. It ended up taking 23 weeks. I was able to survive, though, with so much generous help."

Lee was very private about his situation. Still, members of his congregation at Destiny Church in Grand Island caught wind of his challenges and offered to make sure he had money for the necessities. His car also broke down during that time, and a friend at Ward Laboratories who lived in Cairo, (not far from Grand Island), picked him up and brought him to work every day. Dr. Nick Ward – president of Ward Laboratories and his grandfather, Dr. Ray Ward – who started the business with the late Jolene Ward in the 1980s – found this out and allowed Lee to use the company car.

"I am so grateful. Ward Laboratories became my family. In return, I wanted to treat them like family. I want to return the love I received from them," he said, brimming with gratitude.

"Ward Labs is more than a workplace for me," he reiterated. "I love it here. Now I don't have to have that fear of wondering what I am going to do after a year or two years. I have a future now. I can maybe get married and have a family. I am so happy. Planning a future was so hard in the other scenario. Ward Labs not only provided me with a good job, but they also helped dispel my fears, anxieties, and worries about my future. Now I will do whatever it takes to get the job done."

Lee is up for the job too. Today, as a supervisor, he has his eyes out everywhere for inefficiencies. "I find out what the bottlenecks are and what we can do to make the process faster and better."

Experiencing the "bottlenecks" firsthand in the U.S. immigration system, Lee was more than prepared to work hard and diligently in his role to help make lab systems even better. His helicopter mechanic experience also helped develop some of the skills he needed to work on highly technical equipment in the lab. "If anything is holding back the lab's efficiency, I jump right in and start fixing things. If it's a new instrument, I come up with a method that ensures that instrument can help maximize efficiencies as well."

Today, Lee looks very forward to seeing the parents who encouraged their nervous son to head to the U.S. for new opportunities. "They knew what was best for me. It is my goal to see them every two years once I save up enough vacation time. They will either visit me or I will visit them. I have not seen my family face-to-face since 2018. I hope to see them in 2024. They will be happy, and I will be very happy."

Ward Laboratories is very happy, too. Lee truly cannot thank them enough. "Jordan Westengaard was such a good messenger in this. Without him, and my Ward Laboratories family, I probably would not be here."

A Common Sense, Informed Passion for Soil Health

KERRY HOFFSCHNEIDER | OCTOBER 18, 2023

MARTELL, Neb. – Through reading, learning from others, and hard work, Rod Hollman has actively been implementing practices on his farm and ranch to help renew and regenerate the soil and water. Hollman is very intentional in his quest to share what he has learned and only wishes he had known this information earlier in his agricultural career. Hollman is absolute proof that it is never too late.

"I am passionate about soil health today," he said adamantly. "I am 75 years old, and I want to get the ground better for my grandchildren and great-grandchildren."

Hollman said implementing soil health practices is like starting a healthy workout regimen for the land. "Improving soil health is like body building. You can't go to the gym one day and expect to have muscles the next. It takes time and work to get there."

"Building soil health and soil organic matter takes time and work," he reiterated. "What works for one may not work well for others. It's also important to note that one should not make a change across the board, but should instead try something in one field. If it works, then you can try it on more fields or make a few changes and try again."

"Everyone is free to do what they want to do," Hollman said adamantly, sitting at the dining room table on his dryland Martell, Neb. farm. "My thought is that I wish I would have learned this information 30 years ago. I am going to do what I can today to improve the soil, help the climate, and provide my family better nutrition and try to save money and make an income doing it."

Hollman may regret some of the things he didn't know about soil in the past; however, he does embody a lot of frontline agricultural experience. Hollman was born near Greenwood, Neb. and then moved to the Martell area at an early age where his family were some of the earliest settlers. He farmed all throughout high school. "I was the oldest and could not go out for sports because I was needed to help with the farm."

In 1967, Hollman was drafted and joined the Marine Corps and spent four years serving his nation in the Marine Support Battalion working with the Naval Security Group where he worked with classified military communications. "When I came back home, there was not room to farm with my dad, but I did still have some cows. I had purchased my first registered Angus heifer in 1960 from Earl Bohmont. I had a few cows, rented a bit more pasture, and worked at Goodyear Tire and Rubber Co. in Lincoln, Nebraska and farmed at night."

In 1976 Hollman and his wife, Linda (Bohmont), of Bohmont Herefords, purchased the farm and ranch where they reside today. They eventually started selling registered Angus bulls, mostly private treaty, all across Nebraska to friends and cattlemen from clear away as Thedford. The couple also raised three children who all have full time jobs, but still raise cattle as well. The Hollmans have seven grandchildren and two great-grandsons. In February 2024, Rod and Linda will celebrate their 55th wedding anniversary.

"We have since worked down from 100 cows to about 35," Hollman explained. "In a bad crop year, the cattle carry us."

Hollman said they started as "traditional farmers" who tilled the soil and grew wheat, oats, milo, and soybeans. "Then the corn came in around the 1980s or so and everyone was switching from milo to corn."

Five or six years ago, Hollman's mind about his agricultural practices began to change. "I went to a soil health meeting put on by Randy Pryor, an Extension Agent in Saline County. At the meeting, I began to feel very ignorant about soil. I thought you just fertilized, hoped for rain, and grew a crop. I didn't realize the life that is in the soil. It just opened my eyes. Here I was, almost ready to retire, and I found out I didn't know as much as I thought I did about farming. I didn't know how to do it the right way."

As a result, Hollman continued learning and asking questions. "I didn't know that 95 percent of the life on earth is below the surface of the soil and that you can raise a 200 bushel or more corn crop without applying nitrogen."

Hollman decided to go strictly no-till and to no longer apply anhydrous. "I asked Paul Jasa (UNL Lincoln), 'What does anhydrous do to soil organisms?' Paul told me anhydrous is to soil organisms what nuclear fallout is to people. That really opened my eyes to seeing things differently. Anhydrous is ultimately a form of tillage. When you anhydrous, you are literally using a knife to open the soil up. This goes completely against one of the main factors of soil health that is less, not more, soil disturbance. When you're opening up that furrow, you are letting out the carbon and killing the soil organisms and hurting water infiltration."

Hollman said this type of information became undeniable. "I needed to change."

Numerous examples led him to build his knowledge base, including watching a "Rainfall Simulator Test" that showed the major difference in water infiltration between tilled and no-tilled soil. The Slake test also highly-influenced him to change his mindset. This test uses clumps of different soils immersed in water to show the difference between the aggregates in healthy soil vs. unhealthy soil. Healthy soil won't dissolve as quickly or at all and unhealthy soil will break up completely.

"I went to every soil health conference I could and listened to the experts," he said.

It became increasingly apparent to Hollman that soil health principles are the future of agriculture. These principles he said include:

1. Knowing the context of your unique environment.
2. Keeping the soil covered and undisturbed as often as you can year-ground with cover crops and any plant life that has a continual living root to feed microorganisms and plants.
3. Reducing synthetic inputs or eliminating them entirely.
4. Incorporating grazing livestock of numerous kinds.

"This is not an overnight fix," he noted. "It takes a few years to see results."

In addition to the total elimination of anhydrous from his farming program, Hollman has cut back his nitrogen usage by about 30 percent to about 90 pounds per acre and is striving to do even less. "Also, if you combine this with good soil health practices, you won't have the runoff from farm fields anymore either. Some of the longtime soil health advocates have soil that can absorb 13 inches of rain and not have any runoff. We used to have ditches when I started farming here. We don't have as deep of ditches due to soil erosion and soil erosion is a result of tillage and low soil organic matter."

Soil erosion is serious business, he went on to explain. "Since the Industrial Revolution, the U.S. has lost at least 19 inches of topsoil. The 'Dead Zone' in the Gulf of Mexico is caused by nitrates that leach out of the ground from across the Midwest and other areas and end up there. Dr. Christine Jones out of Australia says a corn plant only uses 10 to 40 percent of nitrogen that is applied to it and the rest goes up to the atmosphere or in our groundwater."

"There is around something like a 100 billion dollars spent annually on synthetic ag inputs like nitrogen and anhydrous," he went on. "Those things don't do the soil any good either. We rely on too many outside sources for our inputs when 78 percent of the atmosphere is already nitrogen, that equates to about 35,000 pounds of nitrogen over every acre that is free! Why not use it? Planting legumes for cover crops and the use of nitrogen fixing bacteria can help this process."

"If you practice soil health practices, there is more water available for the crops, and you can get by on less rainfall," Hollman said adamantly. "I don't know why the irrigators wouldn't want to run their pivots far less, too. It's a proven fact, if you adopt soil health practices, your soil will hold more water."

"Nutrition is also imperative here. Our food and crops have lost much of their nutritional value due to breeding and farming for production and poor soil health. Children have more childhood diseases than two generations ago due to this," he pointed out. "Dr. Christine Jones said the level of nutrition in almost every kind of food has fallen 10 to 100 percent. Now you have to consume twice as much meat, three times as much fruit, and four to five times as many vegetables to obtain the same amount of nutrients as in 1940."

He added a leading nutritionist says that most of our top diseases are due to poor nutrition. "There is a saying that says, 'Healthy Soil = Healthy Food = Healthy People.'"

Hollman would like to see the United States Department of Agriculture (USDA) offer more incentives to farmers and ranchers for implementing regenerative agriculture practices. "If our administrations are going to be so hyped-up on reducing CO_2 emissions for climate change, they need to clearly understand that farming and ranching could take care of a lot of that, using regenerative agricultural practices."

Government programs aren't nearly enough, though, Hollman admitted. That's why he is so passionate about education too. "I went to the President of Doane University, Roger Hughes, and Pete Poppert, head of the Doane ag program and asked them if they would do something on soil health. Students need to learn about agriculture from this vantage point or they will totally miss the important fundamentals – it's not just about growing bushels of crops, it's about people's health and the climate too."

At 75-years-young, Hollman said in many ways he's just starting to really farm and ranch again. He still is finding hope, too, even though from the first of this year to the end of June and beginning of July, his farm only got a couple inches of rain. "We ended up getting some rain the end of June, but then it got hot again, but we still managed to get a crop."

Hollman still hooked up the CASE IH no-till drill he bought, too, "And for those guys who say they can't plant in the trash, this drill will cut through anything. We have to leave that residue on the top to build the soil. That's one of the most important things we can do."

Today, you can find Hollman and his wife continuing to learn and farm corn, soybeans, wheat, and an array of cover crops including frost-seeding red clover in wheat and a host of other experiments to improve their soil health. He also has a vision to continue to improve his cattle herd health through more regenerative practices. "Yes, this year when it comes to rainfall, it's just one we want to leave behind us. But, we're looking forward – because we can't look back."

Looking forward is what farmers and ranchers do in order to make it and it's crystal-clear Hollman won't be giving up anytime soon, either. He wants to relay that optimism for agriculture to his neighbors near and far. "If everyone did what they are supposed to do when it comes to soil health, we wouldn't have the floods and soil erosion and nutritional deficiencies. We would improve upon so many things. But many people are farming the way the tillage companies, some seed companies, and some universities have taught us, and they are making a living doing it that way. But now we have the chance and the resources to unlearn some of that and transition to something better for our environment."

Thank You for Coming Home

KERRY HOFFSCHNEIDER | OCTOBER 10, 2023

Columbus, Neb. – When I found out John Hannah served his nation in Vietnam, I said, "Thank you for your service, John."

John said, "Don't thank me for my service. Thank me for coming home."

Thank you for coming home John, Hannah. There are many reasons to do so. I know you are not alone amongst the Vietnam veterans who feel guilty about coming home when so many did not. We're certainly glad you did come home, though, because you have made such a difference in the world, and you have many more contributions to make. That is why I wanted to interview you.

John Hannah's story...

John Hannah grew up in Southeast Iowa near the little Quaker town of Salem. He was the son of Ben and Jean Hannah. Ben was tragically killed in a truck accident when John was just six years old. When he was in sixth grade, his mom would later marry a kind, hardworking, Swede farmer named Hjalmar Monson.

"I am from the last generation, you know, to hand pick corn, the last people to live like it was in the 1900s. I am among the last that had to run out and pump water in a bucket at the well and use an outhouse full time," Hannah said. "My age group, we're the last of that bunch."

"Dad was killed on Valentine's Day in 1951," Hannah recalled. "When I was young, we lived on the family farm. Mom, who is 99 years old now, always said the farm was kind of a bad deal. It was rundown and such and dad had to fix up all the fences, buildings, house, and this and that. But it was going to be split up with all his brothers and sisters and we weren't going to get anything in an equitable manner, so dad ended up getting a job driving a gasoline semi instead. My dad was away a lot. He had three kids under five years old and was doing everything he could to earn money."

Five years later, when Hannah's mom remarried, it was back to farm life for the family. "My stepfather made it on the farm from the beginning of their marriage to me going to college. But when I went to college, he had to get out. That's when he started working as a paint supervisor at a school bus plant that came into Mt. Pleasant Iowa from Georgia. They were slave drivers, there's not a better way to say it. He was also a heavy smoker and WWII veteran. He was in the Army and landed on the Philippines when MacArthur invaded. From there he went to Okinawa. He never really talked about it much, but I eventually pieced some things together."

When Hannah was in college, he met his wife, Pamala Franks. Pamala's dad was a Marine in WWII, serving in the Pacific, including the dreaded island of Peleliu. "Every Marine knows about Peleliu. When landing on the Pacific Islands, everyone on the first ten boats were likely going to die. Bob Franks was the first guy off the second boat. But he made it."

"Bob also ended up making the original landing on Okinawa. He spoke of traveling across a mile of grass and then coming across a runway. Up in the hills there, east of the runway, they got pinned down and literally dug foxholes to keep safe. For a month, they could not stick their head out of the holes or they were dead," Hannah said. "If you stuck your hand out, there was a good chance you could lose your hand. He survived though. They had no water or food to speak of, but it rained every day, so they would take their ponchos and put it on the edge of the foxhole and the water would run down and collect in their helmets."

Years later, Hannah figured out that his stepfather's Army unit had probably relieved his father-in-law's Marine unit. Neither one of them ever knew that because they never talked about the war, he added.

Hannah started college at Iowa State University in 1962, majoring in entomology. In the spring of 1966, when money for tuition ran out, he joined the Army as a weather observer, serving in New Mexico, and later in Vietnam. After his military service, Hannah earned a Bachelor of Science in entomology in 1971. For the next 12 years, he worked in nursery production as a plant propagator.

Among his many interesting experiences was a summer at Pharr, Texas in 1964 working on a screwworm eradication project at the WWII Air Force base there. "In WWII, after they came up with the atomic bomb, they had all these radioactive products they were trying to find uses for. Well, a researcher/entomologist came up with the idea that you could use radiation to sterilize insects. Then you could grow the sterilized insects and drop them in an airplane and eliminate the unwanted pests."

The eradication project eradicated the screwworm that was wreaking havoc on livestock all across the nation to the tune of $15,000,000 a year in the U.S. back then. "If an animal had a scratch, the screwworms would find it and lay eggs that would hatch and eat a fist-sized hole in the host. My work was to come up with genetic markers that would allow the project to distinguish wild flies from sterile flies."

"Sterilized pupae were air-dropped all over the United States for many years after the project began," he went on to explain. "After a decade or so, the project had eliminated screwworm flies in the U.S. and saved billions of dollars for the country. The U.S. had also helped to get rid of screwworms in Mexico, Panama, and the Caribbean. This all took 15 years or more in the U.S. and was actually a huge government success story no one knows about."

Hannah's career would also take him into seed sales in eastern Iowa in 1983. For 20 years, he then sold seed at wholesale and at other times agronomy product lines at retail. Hannah was later appointed to the Lower Platte North Natural Resources District (NRD) board in 2003 and served for 18 years, including chair of various committees and Chairman of the board of directors. He has also been a part of the Shell Creek Watershed Improvement Group and made farm calls on almost all of the operators in the watershed promoting the adoption of Natural Resource Conservation Service (NRCS) and NRD projects.

Four years ago, Shell Creek became the first watershed in the nation to be delisted for atrazine contamination and still is the only watershed that has been restored. In 2003, Hannah also started Cropdoc, an independent crop consulting business that he has successfully operated to the present.

Hannah is deeply passionate about insects, plants, and all life. He explained why he found a love for entomology during his formative years. "Back when my dad died, my granddad was a well-known carpenter in Salem, Iowa. My grandfather had bought a property in Mt. Pleasant and started building spec houses. When dad died, he had one of those spec houses almost done and we moved into the house which was right next to the country at that time."

"A block away from us there was a barn that used to be the farm," he remembered. "As soon as we got there, I got interested in things that creeped and crawled. I would be excited about everything I saw. I would study the land snails and think, 'Oh this is so cool.' Back in the day, people had way more diversity in their lawns, different sorts of plants and such. There were gardens on nearly every property, lots of flowers, and many trees. Sometime during the fourth or fifth grade, I was really into collecting cool caterpillars. Mom always had dill back then with black swallowtails all over it. I would collect the larvae and hatch them indoors, feeding the things and watching them pupate and make a beautiful chrysalis and then change color and the butterfly would pop out and spread its wings."

"You have to be one heck of a plantsman to be an entomologist. Almost all those little buggers eat plants," Hannah said. "My first job out of college was making baby plants as a plant propagator. Over the years, people came to me often to identify insects or plants."

Hannah can find rich diversity almost everywhere, even at White Sands Missile Range in New Mexico in the Chihuahuan Desert. "Down there, there's all these plants. They are really specialized, nothing like we have up here. I enjoy watching insects and their strange behaviors and life stories. It's fascinating what you see, even in the desert."

"When we moved to Nebraska, I could sniff out a prairie a million miles away," he said.

Today Hannah is concerned because so much has changed. "Here I sit today in Columbus, Nebraska, and you can look clear out on the horizon in many places, like it's an ocean. There may be an elevator out there like a ship on the ocean, but there's not much plant and insect diversity anymore. It's like being in the worst desert imaginable, worse than the sandiest spot in the world, in Saudi Arabia or the Sahara in many ways."

"We have taken out all the fences where there used to be chokecherry, elm, locust trees, plum thickets, and even wildflowers. Most of the fritillaries, a beautiful butterfly species, are gone along with other butterflies and insects. The predominant plants are corn, soybeans, and brome grass and not much else. So, I look at how much things have changed, and I think to myself, 'This is an abomination.' Human beings are becoming an unfit species by letting our natural systems collapse. We are like dinosaurs in that way, waiting for a meteorite to finish the job. They apparently became an unfit species and were in decline millions of years before their extinction. If we don't recognize what is happening with our environment and make adjustments, we will earn the same fate as dinosaurs. And buying more air conditioners is not the solution."

"What I am saying is, there are other ways out there and life will be better if we change," Hannah said. "We have the warning signs, plenty of them. We're essentially 'crapping in our own nest.'"

Hannah believes there is hope if farmers start changing and only they can lead the way, he said confidently. "We're not moving the needle enough. Our water nitrate issues are getting measurably worse, not better, in many areas. I know this for a fact in the Lower Platte North NRD. And there are soil erosion issues almost everywhere."

He thinks it's going to take sweeping agricultural practice changes like no-till and other regenerative approaches that save, preserve, and renew the soil and water resources. "Where's the hope? The hope in the story is that I do know there are at least an embarrassingly few farmers who are really doing it right. Their land is not losing any soil or water and they are soaking in every inch of rain, even if they have a five-inch downpour. There are people out there doing it really right, but there aren't as many as there should be or needs to be."

Hannah compliments the ones doing the right thing. But, he said, so often they have to watch their neighbor's soil wash away in gullies. "So often farms literally right next to each other are in stark contrast – one farm with water sitting on top of it and running off and the other farm soaking all the moisture in."

"It's going to sound harsh, but if we're really going to have hope, we have to look at the biological side of things and work with that. We have huge carbon storage potential in our farm soils. We should not tolerate nitrate and chemical levels increasing in our groundwater given the present concern for impacts like cancer rates," he noted.

"We need more pollinators unless we plan to eat porridge the rest of our lives," he added. "Present subsidies encourage people to do the wrong things. Subsidizing ethanol favors one crop over another, leading to supply distortions. Subsidizing crop insurance gives incentives for plowing up the few remaining prairies, pastures, and wetlands. We need to get animals back on the land and graze them instead of concentrating them as a pollution source. We should conserve and build our soil resources."

Hannah relayed a recent story he read about the west coast of Ireland where there is an area with just a little skin of grass atop rock. "Archaeologists have discovered that area used to be farmed 6,000 years ago. The farmers created soil loss, just like we are doing in the United States today. The soil disappeared along with the farmers and today, 6,000 years later, it is one of the largest wilderness areas in Ireland and still not farmable. The area became completely vacated, never to be farmed or populated again."

"We don't have to get to that point," Hannah said adamantly. "We have the information and examples to do better than that and a lot of that is in the idea of regenerative agriculture."

Thank you, John, for coming home. Thank you for making a difference and being a voice of reason in a world that is losing its soil and freshwater resources by the second. As you state, the hope is we absolutely can build soil again and, as a result, bring back the bugs, butterflies, grazing animals, families, and all life. We're not done hearing from Mr. Hannah and his network, either. He is going to connect us to a farmer friend or two he knows that are doing the right thing. We can't wait to keep learning. That's what the Graze Master Group is about, learning, from each other and Balancing Nature & Profitability. We absolutely know we can do this after talking to people like John.

His Name is Gail
– The Recovering Conventional Farmer

Kerry Hoffschneider | September 7, 2023

"Hello, my name is Gail, and I am a recovering conventional farmer." "This is how I usually start my talks," Gail Fuller said. "Sometimes it takes a little bit, but then they usually get it and reply (in the spirit of a self-help group), 'Hi Gail.'"

Gail Fuller is one of my heroes and that is why I was so excited he agreed to take some time and talk with me. I said, "Gail, I want you to talk to the farmers in my area. I think they work hard. I think many of them really care, and they just don't know about a better way. I think they have something really good in them to offer. But right now, they are getting worn out."

"I understand," Fuller said. "I was right where they are."

Gail's Story

Gail Fuller grew up just north of Emporia, Kan. on the Neosho River. "The inner child in me had known all my life that we were farming wrong. But it took me from 1979 to 2003 to really start to question things."

Fuller was always a hardworking farmer, dedicated to his tasks. In 2000 he was farming 3,200 acres of Roundup Ready® corn and soybeans. "I was the fourth largest farmer in my county. But I came to know a change was needed."

"All farmers, I think in some fashion, grow up with a conservationist mindset," he said. "There was the little creek behind my parents' house where we would look for raccoon tracks, you know, all of those things farm kids do. And with those experiences, grew my affection for the trees, wildlife, and all those things."

"But then, when I became a farmer, suddenly we needed insecticides and those insecticides could kill some of the birds and insects too, but there I was needing to make money and 'grow corn to feed the world,'" Fuller admitted. "The government had a big role to play in this mindset change. They quit talking about farmers as producers of food and changed the language from food to commodities. I think that language desensitized us into using all the chemicals."

A change of heart

"I knew we were farming wrong because I hated to see the soil erosion," he recalled. "I knew tillage was wrong, but in 1979 that is about all we had. We tried no-till in the mid-1980s, but we failed miserably, mostly because I was young, and I wasn't going to ask for help. I was too stubborn to ask the neighbor no-tilling successfully how he was doing it.

So, we went back to tillage."

Then, from 1993 to 1995, Fuller said, "There were some horrible years for a river rat. We had seven floods in those few years. When the flood hit in 1993, I had about 40 acres of ground chiseled before the floods hit and I lost eight inches of topsoil off all the ground that was tilled. That was the last time we tilled."

Fuller changed to no-till and didn't look back. But no-till wasn't an overnight success. "The no-till experts said in three years we would see things improve, the earthworm populations improve, and yields getting better. But in 2000, we had very few earthworms and our yields were going down and the erosion was not getting better."

Unwilling to give up, Fuller kept learning, "At that time we were in a corn and soybean rotation and 70 percent of the corn was chopped for silage because two of my biggest landowners were feedlots. What we were doing was removing all the carbon from the soil. In 2003, we decided to put wheat into the rotation and had an 'ah-ha moment.' The wheat succeeded, even with all the excuses that you can't grow wheat in Eastern Kansas. By 2004, wheat was my number one cash crop."

"I realized it was about the carbon," Fuller said adamantly. "I also realized the soil was meant to be alive! The universities at that time for the most part didn't talk about the soil microbiome, earthworms, nutritious food, or any of those things. It was about planting seeds in the dirt and amending the dirt with whatever crap the industry wanted to sell us so the industry could make a profit."

A STEEP LEARNING CURVE

"It was a really steep learning curve. Absolutely," Fuller said. "But it was a lot of fun. No-Till on the Plains was a big benefit for me. I planted my first cover crop in 1996 on small acreages until 2000 and they honestly weren't working. We got dry and simply stopped planting the cover crops. It was that successful wheat crop in 2003 when everything clicked instantly. That was when we really learned what a cover crop was supposed to be doing."

"A big part of all the fun was also all the life! All I had ever been taught to do was kill things," Fuller said passionately. "Suddenly I get to talk about encouraging life on the farm."

THE CROP INSURANCE CONUNDRUM

Everything was clicking, but government policy wasn't one of those things. Fuller had faced a series of challenges, but, he said, "Crop insurance was the one I couldn't handle, and it cost me my farm."

It all went down in 2012, the second driest year on record at the time. "I was denied my crop insurance claim due to 'mismanagement of cover crops.' We were literally less than a week from having to sell our cattle herd due to the drought, because we had nothing for them to eat except waist-high corn. They (crop insurance agents) looked at our corn and saw it full of weeds and cover crops because the chemicals did not work because it was too hot and dry. I had records that we had tried to spray chemicals three times, and nothing worked."

At the time, Fuller was the first farmer to implement cover crops in Kansas and the farm bureaucracy wasn't ready for the frontrunner ahead of his time. "Cover crops complicated their lives and made it harder for the agents to do their jobs. I understood that. So, they threw the water on the fire before it got started."

Yet again, facing a bureaucratic barrier didn't stop Fuller from forging ahead. From 2012 to 2013 it was far from easy, but they were making serious headway with a focus on soil health and all life on the farm. By then, they were back to a five-year rotation on the farm with 15 different cash crops, everything from barley, to sunflowers, wheat, triticale, and all sorts of cover crops.

"Our organic matter had exploded too. We had a lot of failures, but the successes were financially rewarding, and we were stabilizing the farm financially and environmentally. We had 1.7 to 3 percent organic matter across the farm in 2000 and in 2014 we were between four and seven percent organic matter. My infiltration rates on my worst soil were six inches per hour," he said.

Back in 2005, Fuller had met the love of his life. She would also bring a lot of success to the farm. "Lynnette had grown up on a large cow/calf ranch. She didn't understand the row crop side of things, but had grown up atop a horse in the flint hills, with all the wildflowers and diversity around. One night, early on when we were dating, I was still an 'in the closet' cover cropper. She asked me, 'You have to tell me what you are doing in the fields behind the trees.' Ninety minutes later of me talking, I looked up at the clock and said to myself, 'Oh no, this is the end of this relationship.' But it wasn't the end, instead she said, 'Gail, that all makes sense. Why aren't you doing this on all your acres?' That gave me the confidence to think, 'Why aren't I doing this on all my acres?' From there, the farm just exploded."

His dad was getting it too, Fuller recalled, "My dad had semi-retired by that point, and he still loved to cut wood. My brother and I told him he could cut wood, but someone had to be with him. So, he hired someone. This individual was with him all the time and had observed what was going on around the farm for some time, too. The 'hired companion for dad' also noticed Lynnette really brought a lot of additional life to the farm with her chickens, sheep, and livestock background."

Fuller's dad also noticed something when he was with his son one day. "I will admit, there is a difficulty associated with growing all those cash crops. You have to have a market for them before you buy the seed because a lot of elevators won't take them. We were grazing some of them, too. We were growing everything from barley to mung beans and cowpeas. Some of the crops were being sold as cover crop seed. The first year we planted barley my dad was helping to fill the drill and he was losing his eyesight by then. I thought he might not notice it wasn't wheat seed we were pouring into the drill. He did notice, though, and asked, 'Are you going to harvest this or is it one of those cover crops for a seed company?' Then dad said, 'You know, barley makes really good feed. It was one of my favorite crops.' I asked him why he stopped planting it. He said, 'I don't know.'"

Slammed in 2012

It was okay his dad didn't remember why he stopped growing barley, Fuller said. "We had all forgotten why we did what we did. It was time for a lot of changes and remembering what we had done in the past that actually worked."

The horrible drought year of 2012 just wouldn't let up, though, and in the midst of everything, Fuller was researching something else he had some growing reservations about – glyphosate. "I was using more Roundup® as a no-tiller than many of my neighbors and because of that usage I was also the first one to have resistant weeds. Then I started hearing how glyphosate could be bad for you. But everyone on my 'team' was saying those people were tree hugger liberals that shouldn't talk with their mouths full."

Fuller proceeded with his research and eventually attended a meeting where Dr. Jill Clapperton, a rhizosphere ecologist, spoke about the dangers of glyphosate. He also ran across Dr. Don Huber, a plant physiologist, who had also done a lot of research on the dangers of glyphosate. "I listened to a video interview with Dr. Huber and that's when I heard him say glyphosate is an antibiotic."

Glyphosate is an antibiotic

Those words hit home – hard. "I am sitting there at 11:30 at night on the farm where I am implementing cover crops and all these crop rotations and grazing livestock, and we were all about the soil microbes and there I was spraying antibiotics on the crops a couple times a year. I thought to myself, 'What am I doing to my farm and my health?' If glyphosate is an antibiotic, it is killing our gut health. I had been lied to or misinformed by my entire team – the bankers, seed salespeople, marketers, extension agents, so many people had assured me how safe this all was."

A legal battle

2012 continued to be the year that wouldn't end. The crop insurance blow he is certain he was targeted for, also came to a head. "At the same time I was learning about glyphosate, I was heading into a 20-month battle over my crop insurance. At this time, I immediately lost my operating line of credit. We were down to 1,800 acres at that point. With no line of credit and 1,800 acres, there was no way we were going to farm for two years. It was a financial disaster. I was also stopping the use of Roundup® and the custom applicators didn't want to work with me. The neighboring farmers were taking ground away from me and I was losing friends."

Still, Fuller won the case. "My crop insurance denial letter had arrived on October 29, 2012, and my arbitration hearing was on April Fool's Day – 2014. I made sure the arbitrator understood how fitting that day was."

During this legal battle process, they sensed the opposition was changing the cause of denial midstream. Fuller prepared his second defense and the opposition did end up changing their cause of denial. "We argued the first cause of denial and we argued they could not change their cause of denial midstream. Then, for what it's worth, we won all three cases."

What it's worth, is a powerful story that lives on, nation and worldwide, because a farmer didn't quit. "For me it was a victory. Because of my case, the rules for crop insurance started to be overhauled and that was a big win for other farmers. Well, for me, I was broke."

Broke, but not broken

"The good side of this is that Lynnette and I had been discussing downsizing the farm even further. I don't know if we would have done so if they hadn't tried to push me out," he admitted.

In 2014, Fuller quit using the crop insurance program. "We were around 1,300 acres at that point with no line of credit."

In 2014, any joy of winning the case was erased by his brother's death in a farm accident. "The depression hit hard. My mental state eroded terribly without me knowing it in a lot of ways."

"It was a rough, rough time across the board. Lynnette was a lifesaver. Even my kids, understandably so, were questioning me," he went on. "I lost friends. I couldn't go to the parts store or anywhere. I walked with my head down because either someone was talking about me, or I owed someone."

Endings and new beginnings

"In 2018, I knew we were nearly done. It took me a year to convince Lynnette, the bank, and my parents that I could not come up with another good business plan that would work," he said. "In 2019, we decided to sell the house and farm. We had a realtor lined up. This was right before we were holding a Fuller Field School on the farm. Dr. Zach Bush was one of the speakers and we decided to put the sale on hold for a month to host the event."

"Zach's opening statement at Fuller Field School was, 'All cancer is caused by stress. If you have stress in your life, you have to let it go.' I think deep down I put the farm sale on hold using the field school as an excuse, hoping for a million-dollar lottery check or something in the mail. I remember after the event was over, Lynnette and I were in bed, and I thought she was asleep. Then, in the dark I heard her say, 'Did you hear Zach?' I said, 'I did, I will call the agent tomorrow.'"

A FARM SALE AND HOPE FOR THE FUTURE

"The next day the farm was up for sale. We left 57 years of blood, sweat, and tears and moved. We had nothing left. We used a capital gains 1031 exchange so we could buy a piece of property and continue to farm. When you're broke, you're broke," he said.

The couple moved to a 162-acre farm outside of Severy, Kan. "Now we are in the process of putting our lives back together and healing on a new farm."

The new farm has the same love for farming envisioning its future, too. "We direct-market grass-finished beef and lamb, pastured-pork, chicken, and duck. We are trying to keep the small orchards alive with the extreme weather patterns going on. And, we have been in a drought since we've been here, too. Mother Nature is still in charge. But it's a lot more fun being broke and eating a lot of good food than drinking a case of Pepsi like I used to drink every day and being miserable."

They aren't giving up. They're healthier and helping others, holding healing workshops focused on nutrition and mental health. Lynnette also has found her dream job with Jonathan Lundgren at the Ecdysis Foundation, all while she helps keep everything on the farm going. In her off-farm career, she is helping spread the good news about a better way of farming in tandem with nature.

The couple is making it all go for as long as they can, just like they always have. Fuller said everyone really can make a change for the better. "I think we all need to stand up and be the revolution we need to be. I beg farmers to take back their lives, their families, and their farms."

Thank you, Gail and Lynnette, from the bottom of my heart, for your courage. I know this story will change a farm for the better. I just know it.

Learn more: www.fullerfieldschool.com

Farm Foreclosures and Legacy

Kerry Hoffschneider | September 4, 2023

Drawing by Nebraska artist Micah Moulin, Moulin Farm Art and Repair.

There was once a farm and then there was a memory. Yes indeed, you find out what a farm is made of when you see the foreclosure sign go up. You find out what the farmer is made of, too. You find out about life and what really matters.

My cousin Micah Moulin works hard in his day job. He also knows tractors inside and out. In his spare time, Micah's hobby is drawing. The amateur artist practices whenever and wherever he can. He practices because he loves to draw. Micah is not unlike the farmer in this way. Most often the farmer farms or the rancher ranches because they love to. That labor of love becomes a lifestyle, not just a place to go to work. A farm is a family. A farm is also a story and sometimes the farm part of the story is forced to end. When the foreclosure sign arrives, more than a farm dies.

Micah clearly understands the living and dying lessons that happen on a farm. He understands them so much that he reached out to me recently and said he was camping and drawing. He's working on a new series of artwork depicting the challenges associated with agriculture. He asked if I would write about this particular drawing, and I agreed.

I immediately knew the topic I was going to cover. Just in time for Labor Day, we have a farm foreclosure. But let me tell you, the work was not wasted, even when all is seemingly lost. Because it's not about the farm, it's about who is watching the farmer and what they see and also how they feel as they face life's most difficult moments.

Farms aren't foreclosed on because farmers don't work hard enough. They are lost for a variety of reasons. In the 1980s, many farms were lost because everything changed literally overnight. They didn't lose farms because they hadn't fed the hogs, harvested the crops or put-up hay. They didn't lose farms because they didn't pray enough at dinnertime or can enough from the garden. They often lost the farm because a system set up to fail them, failed them.

What I absolutely love amidst the tragedy of this drawing is the man standing with his arm around the son. I can only imagine the tears. I can only imagine the pain associated with a loss this tremendous, even shame. But what the man in this photo clearly recognizes is that while they are watching tractors chained up and driven away, he is touching what is most important about the farm anyway – the future standing next to him.

We talk a lot about legacy when we buy more land, but the real legacy of our lives isn't the land at all. The real legacy is the love we have for people who matter deeply to us and for our neighbors all around us, here and across the globe. The real legacy is ensuring the gifts within people have the conditions to become fruitful, not fruitful for the sake of wealth alone, but fruitful because of what those gifts displayed can do to make the world a better place.

It's true, sometimes we get to work on farms and sometimes those same farms work us over. Sometimes, the seemingly most successful farmer is also the most miserable. Miserable because they forgot what really matters on a family farm – the farm family.

There is opportunity in this drawing. There is also hope. There is a relationship intact between a father and son that can suffer this loss together, but also envision something new. We don't know what that new will be for them, but we can imagine it. We can offer encouraging words and a hug. The farmer in the photo is not looking down, he's looking ahead. His son needs to see him looking confidently into a future beyond a foreclosure. A future that absolutely does exist.

If we're going to have fewer farm foreclosures, we're going to have to figure out what really matters most on the farm and why we're doing what we are doing. If we don't take the time to find out the dreams of the people working with us to keep the farm going, we're not a successful farm. I don't care how many acres you have. I do care how many hearts feel valued and treasured there. I do care if they feel heard. I do care about an environment that fosters and embraces the free flow of ideas and not fear.

Today is Labor Day – it's a day when we are supposed to rest from our labors. It's a very good day to put your arm around a person you love, because we're supposed to love the people more than the farm anyway. That's what life is all about. Farms come and go. They are as fleeting and fickle as the paperwork we fill out to "own" them for such a minuscule amount of time in the whole schematic of time.

What can't be replaced ever again are people. They matter. Get to know them. Get to know their hearts and then you'll know how to face any challenge side by side. Yes, even facing a farm foreclosure can mean a new start, even something better maybe. Sometimes the closure part is an open door to the future and what you make of it. And make it you can – together.

Follow Micah at: www.facebook.com/moulinfarmartandrepair

Homeland Ties

Kerry Hoffschneider | August 25, 2023

Deb Echo-Hawk and Del Ficke.

When Del Ficke was a child, his Grandfather Adolph Ficke would take him to the old Pawnee camp site near Pleasant Dale, Neb. many times and tell him a story about a cold, challenging winter in the late-1800s. Adolph heard the story from his father, H.F. Ficke, many times as well and was told to ensure it was passed on for generations to come. That story led to a reconnection between the Pawnee Nation and the Ficke family and a sacred blue corn harvest that goes far beyond seed.

"The story went like this, varying in versions each time he repeated it," Ficke began. "In the winter of 1869, my great-great-grandfather, Johann Ficke, homesteaded on a hill overlooking Middle Creek less than a mile away from where the Pawnee had their camp. It was a harsh winter and the Fickes, with the limited provisions that many pioneers had in those days, were facing great difficulty. The Pawnee fed my ancestors during that very cold winter and my Grandfather told me without their help, they would have most likely died."

The history of the Pawnee and their removal is outlined by Roger Echo-Hawk, a member of the Pawnee Nation, in a paper he wrote, *Settling the Land Between Two Rivers*. "The vast majority of the Pawnees were removed to Oklahoma in two groups in 1873 and 1874. The third (and last) group of Pawnees left Nebraska in late 1875 under the leadership of Baptiste Bayhylle. This final group consisted mainly of Skidis ... The Pawnees came together on their new reservation in Oklahoma in 1876."

Separated from the fertile soils of their Nebraska homeland, the Pawnee people carried their seed with them. But, the soils of Oklahoma were different, and their seeds were not acclimated there. The Pawnee Nation lost not only their homeland, but much of their ability to grow the seeds they loved.

Fast forward to 2003 when Ronnie O'Brien, an instructor at Central Community College in Hastings, Neb., reached out to Deb Echo-Hawk, the Keeper of the Seed for the Pawnee Nation. O'Brien was seeking information about Pawnee history and seed preservation. Today (as of the writing of the article in 2019), the Pawnee Seed Preservation Project has grown to around 20 growers across Nebraska, that now include Ficke and his family and his cousin Gregg Eggerling.

"I met Deb Echo-Hawk, Electa Hare-Redcorn, and Ronnie O'Brien at a presentation about the Pawnee Seed Preservation Project and approached them about planting some of their seeds for them. I was honored they trusted me enough to take part in the project," Ficke explained. "That's how it all started. I began planting seeds three years ago. It was an opportunity to make a small difference in the face of all the wrongs that had been done to their people."

In 2018, Del and Brenda Ficke delivered the largest harvest of Pawnee Sacred Blue Corn to the Pawnee Nation in Oklahoma in 125 years.

"We have thoroughly enjoyed the group of Pawnee who return to Nebraska every year for the harvest. I know it is difficult for them to make the trip here. We were honored to deliver the corn to them in Oklahoma, too. They are our family."

"We greatly appreciate the chance to reunite with the Ficke family again," Deb Echo-Hawk said. "This reunion and friendship aids and enhances all that the Pawnee Seed Preservation Project stands for in our world today."

"Traditional foods are more than healthy foods, they are part of the history, land, culture, and spiritual practice of a people – health, as well as part of the economic fabric of a tribe," Deb went on. "Traditional foods are part of the generational heritage passed on from elders. Our friendship assures us that the future will be formed out of simplistic means that will bring food to the table. All the growers in this project are so important to us and we thank them. It's about keeping homeland ties."

Ficke said, "My goal was to get enough that every Pawnee could at least taste some of their blue corn and help connect them to their sacred traditions. Growing this corn for the Pawnee is a very small thank you."

Website: www.pawneeseed.org
Facebook: www.facebook.com/pawneeseedpreservationsociety

My God, My Family, and My Art

Kerry Hoffschneider | July 21, 2023

CARRIE JOHNSON AT HER FARMHOUSE WINDOW WITH HER EASEL AND BRUSH.

The mother of five gets a second to stand at her easel. She lifts up a plate covering some dried-up acrylic paint. "I will get back to it, but the summer has been busy. The children are home, and family comes first."

Family is everything for Carrie Johnson, who is nestled with her five children in a farmhouse she and her husband refurbished themselves located near Friend, Neb. "Everything around here may not seem like much to some, but we've earned it all and it's our home."

Home is picturesque rural living – a few horses, farm dogs, pastures, fields all around, and happy children meeting you at the door. The only boy in the family jumps on the trampoline with his jeans and a western belt on, anxious for dad to come home so they can head to Cheyenne, Wyo. for adventures with their horses. The oldest is making eggs for breakfast and the other girls run around playing.

Johnson met her husband when he was a horse trainer for her parents on their farm in Kansas. "There were five kids in the family on our multigenerational farm. The biggest thing we learned was work ethic – walking milo and beans and cleaning out the hog houses. On the farm I learned about not giving up, how to keep going, and problem solving."

She also learned creativity. Her parents demonstrate their artistic talents to this day. "Dad is an immaculate woodworker and mom is a great painter."

Johnson's artistic interests were further inspired by a high school art teacher. "She became my heroine. The relationship actually began because she had a daughter born with a major brain injury and she trusted me to babysit her. She taught me how to really love someone. She also taught me about art and to look at it as problem solving instead of just talent. She taught me things different from farm life."

After high school, Johnson headed to Lawrence, Kan. to earn her degree in Fine Arts and Illustration. At age 20, she headed to Paris by herself, something she was told Kansas farm girls just don't do. Still, away she flew. "You could get cheap rates as a student, and I went over spring break and took an extra week for travel. The hotel rooms were cheap, and I walked around everywhere. While I was there, the art workers were on strike, so I didn't see the Louvre, but I did see the Versailles gardens, explored cemeteries, and was in awe of the oldness of everything there. America has so much made out of plastic and not built to last. There is a delayed sense of gratification there. Things that last take time."

Upon graduating, Johnson was off traveling again. "For a mission trip, I created 40 illustrations that incorporated Bible stories. My target audience was North African Muslims. I traveled to Morocco to see their art so I could reflect their style in my pieces. I liked Spain even more than France because they were such a colorful, laid-back, and fun people. I definitely want to go back."

But for now, she is completely content at home fulfilling her favorite role in the world – mom. "I always dreamed of living in a rural community, raising kids, and doing art. For nearly 20 years, I threw most of my art stuff in a drawer and didn't touch it. I expressed my creativity in raising kids, gardening, and decorating my house. But then I started thinking about the empty hole inside and I needed an outlet doing something very special to me. So, I decided to drop a few things and start painting again."

"I paint mostly nature and I always ask myself – 'How can I use my art to glorify God?' I want to glorify God in everything I do. I see God in where we live – rural landscapes with unbounding freedom ring in my heart. I enjoy painting birds, fields, flowers, and also images of the Midwest and western portions of the U.S."

"I read *Art of the West* magazine and always think, 'Those are my people. They love nature and see creating as a reflection of God.' God is a great artist and in nature I see His art. I don't worship nature, I appreciate it. The most beautiful places in North America are places like the Grand Canyon, Montana, and the open prairie. I feel claustrophobic in the cities. Here it feels free."

"I also feel like what you have been exposed to or what is in your heart comes out in your art," she went on.

What is in Johnson's heart also comes out through her photography business. She wants to take photos of families for an affordable price, and she has a mission. "It's called *Jentry's Light Photography*. Our first baby lived only three days and was very premature. We took pictures of the baby and I had them developed. When I went to pick them up, the girl who gave me the pictures was dressed in Goth fashion, and was visibly moved by the images. She told me, 'I can see Jesus in these pictures.'

That's what it's about. Anytime I can glorify God, I am so happy."

"Through my photos, I want to keep families together," Johnson said. "I want to showcase what a beautiful blessing children are. I am also able to share Jentry's story and that way her story can live on. When we lost Jentry, I went through three years of depression. I have spoken to a lot of other mothers who have lost their children this way, too. I hope I can help in some small way."

"Our tears are never wasted," Johnson added with confidence. "God never wastes our pain. I can see many ways that pain was used for His glory. I tell people all the time that it's very hard to lose a baby. But, at the same time, I know the first thing Jentry opened her eyes to was the face of Jesus. There is nothing more precious than that."

Johnson is ready to return to her painting. When she can spare 30 minutes or so, you can picture her in the light of the farmhouse window, standing at an easel adorned with vines and birds she painted in acrylic to decorate the spot where all her pieces lean and wait to come to life.

Other artists are also a great inspiration for her, like the Impressionist painter Berthe Morisot. "She was a mom, too, who died saving her baby's life. A lot of her artwork is of mothers and babies. She inspires me. She was the mom of a bunch of kids and also an artist whose work ended up in the Louvre and is there to this day."

Most of all, Johnson wants her art to leave an impression on the rural people and places she loves so much, "Our creativity was made by God. My goal is to bring joy to other people and worship God with my art. Yes, I had to put my art on the back burner a bit, but family comes first. I am looking forward to this coming school year when Clara lies down for her nap, and I get to paint."

Follow Johnson's heart for God, family, and art at:
www.facebook.com/JentrysLightPhotography/

Regenerative Agriculture Holds Promise for Next Generation

Kerry Hoffschneider | April 12, 2023

Davis and Lori Behle are pursuing their dreams in regenerative agriculture.

Davis Behle said when your eyes are opened to regenerative agriculture, there's opportunity everywhere you look. "It all takes education, because it's against mainstream thinking. It takes people coming alongside you to show you why they are passionate about doing things a different way."

The path to "regenerative agriculture" is one that can begin to be found in the six principles of soil health. On paper, it's a list – minimizing or eliminating soil disturbance, increasing plant diversity, keeping living roots in the soil as much as possible and introducing livestock back to the land. In reality, these principles play out in a variety of contexts across the nation and the world.

Behle credits Del Ficke of *Ficke Cattle Company* and the co-founder of the Graze Master Group for being the first to introduce him to these concepts during a trip to his farm during college. "Del Ficke was the first person who told me about soil health. I drove out and met him and we dug up some soil and had a lot of good discussion around that. That's when I really started to get a hold of that version of agriculture."

The seeds of agriculture were also sown in Behle's life early on growing up northwest of Kearney. Both his parents had grown up on farms and introduced Behle to 4-H and a love for the land early on. The couple also served rural areas in their professional careers. His mom, Christie, worked coordinating services for young children with developmental disabilities. His father, Dave, was employed with a rural electric company.

"We had a pasture up the road where we were able to have cattle," Behle explained. "It started with bucket calves and then dairy heifers. Then we bought a pair of Angus heifers from my great uncle's dispersion sale. That's when we started a little Angus herd and began showing breeding beef and market steers. I loved getting to work with my dad and taking care of the cattle. It was a lot of fun."

Behle continued gaining more ag experiences with his involvement in 4-H and working for local farmers that attended church with the family. After high school, he attended the University of Nebraska–Lincoln and pursued an Agribusiness degree and an entrepreneurship minor with the Engler program.

"My first job out of college was at Alturas Ranches in northeastern California," he recalled.

"This wasn't the part of California with palm trees and beaches. It was the high desert with one blinking stoplight in the county. My wife Lori and I had gotten married halfway through my senior year of college and as I was nearing graduation, a mentor recommended I go somewhere and experience agriculture in a different setting. Alturas was one of the ranches he was connected with, and he pointed me in that direction."

California ranch life afforded Behle a host of firsthand experiences, everything from baling hay, to harvesting wild rice, moving cattle and planting cover crops. The couple was also able to travel around the state to see all sorts of types of farming and crops – pistachios, almonds, stone fruit, strawberries, tomatoes, and more. "It was really eye-opening and neat to see all those different cropping systems."

Various office responsibilities also fell under his list of duties. He would conduct software-related work, put together presentations as well as conduct field by field analysis, explore new business opportunities and do grant writing, as well. During his time there, he was also charged to reach out to Green Cover Seed. "We were following the work of the Savory Institute and my boss asked me to find cover crops to experiment with. That's when I connected with Green Cover."

Behle and his wife always intended to return to Nebraska one day and were able to do so when a temporary position became available to work with the Rathje family at Windy Ridge Simmentals near Seward, Neb. This provided four or five months of flex time for Behle to explore his career options. Among the job interviews during this time included an opportunity with Green Cover Seed and today he is employed full time with the company.

"I really enjoy getting to work with people all over the country and helping them achieve their goals. It's really more about education than anything else," he admitted when it comes to introducing regenerative practices and delving into cover crops.

Behle and Lori recently relocated near Arlington, Neb. after they bought Lori's grandpa's farm. They are thrilled to have the honor of currently owning 10 acres and plan to purchase 150 more acres in the future. Planting their roots in the area and getting to know people is important to the couple. "Lori's Grandpa Bob was also an entrepreneur who grew crops outside the norm, and I want to carry on that legacy as well."

This is the fun, experimental phase, Behle said. "This year's theme is to try and fail at as many things as possible so we can find out what we're interested in, what we're good at, and what is economically feasible."

Davis sees an abundance of opportunities on the farm and wants to find some more direct to consumer or other niche ways of marketing what they grow. Ideas include everything from seed crops, food grade grains, market produce, cut flowers, eggs, and perhaps even an orchard. "Our goal is to grow the farm in a regenerative, diversified way."

"I really enjoy helping efforts to grow the regenerative ag community. It feels like a win-win in most ways when you start looking at agriculture this way," Behle said with confidence. "The economics over time of the regenerative path leads to a better future for the farmers, consumers, and the entire planet. I feel very passionate about regenerative agriculture, and I think there is a lot of curiosity out there. Sometimes in the Midwest people feel bad or hesitant about asking for help, myself included, but I want to continue to help people to find more opportunities where they can learn and ask questions."

Urban Farming a Labor of Love

KERRY HOFFSCHNEIDER | APRIL 11, 2023

AMANDA STRUBLE IN FRONT OF SHELVES FILLED TO THE BRIM WITH THE FRUITS OF HER FAMILY'S LABOR.

When hail pummeled the community of Utica, Neb. last summer, the siding on many homes was shredded, shingles were tattered, and windows were broken all over town. The Struble house didn't escape the storms either, but replacing battered exterior walls wasn't the most important next step on the family's list – replanting the garden came first.

Gardening is an understatement for Amanda Struble and her husband Josh's "urban farm" that spans nearly every inch of their backyard and a good portion of their front yard, too. For them, it's about love for the land and growing food for their family and extra to share. It's also about protecting all natural resources and trying hard not to be wasteful. "The boys love catching rainwater. They get excited about how much water they get in their buckets."

"Even the landscaping is edible," she admitted. "I want the land to all be useful and I don't like bare spaces. Anytime you see bare ground, a weed will come. The weeds are telling us something, that ground wants to be covered. Bare ground will always try to heal itself if we don't have something growing on it."

Struble has literally covered a lot of ground with her green thumb and also in her journeys throughout life. She developed her industrious ways growing up near Fullerton, Neb. where her parents – Vern and Cindy Olson – operated a diversified farm. "On the livestock front, we had beef cows, sheep, and when I was very little, we had pigs. At one point, we had 200 ewes and were lambing out every year. We also had Angora goats and my sister got Boer goats in high school. There were turkeys, ducks, broilers, laying hens, rabbits, cats, and a dog of course, too."

"On the crop side, dad raised corn, soybeans, and alfalfa," she went on. "He planted a field of sunflowers one year, too, so there was a whole bin of sunflower seeds that we fed the chickens. We lived along Highway 14 and dad said he planted the sunflowers because people needed something different to look at when they drove down the highway."

Cindy went to school to be a nurse, but management duties on the farm and raising a family became priority. "Mom truly worked on the farm. She did a lot of the management, the bookwork, and was a major part of farm operations, helping with lambing season and working in the fields. She has beautiful handwriting and was always making lists. Her nursing came in handy working with the livestock, and I remember during softball one season all of the players were so hot, mom sprung into action. She knew exactly what to do in situations like that."

"I always say we lived in the middle of everywhere and nowhere,"

Struble commented about rural life. "We went to school in Fullerton, church in Genoa, St. Edward to the doctor, Albion to 4-H, Cedar Rapids for youth group, and Belgrade had a bar, restaurant, and a convenience store – I remember the bus would sometimes stop there and the kids who were still on would get to go inside and pick something out."

When Struble was a senior, her dad decided to pursue an entirely new direction in life and headed to the seminary to become a Methodist minister. Her parents stayed on the farm for as long as they could, but with less help they eventually sold the farm and moved to St. Edward. By the time her father retired, he was leading four parishes.

After graduating, Struble headed to Southeast Community College in Lincoln. "There I realized my whole life up to that point had been teaching in some way – in places like 4-H and Sunday School – so I transferred to the University of Nebraska to pursue teaching. I always had a love for agriculture, so I went through the Ag Education program."

During this time, Struble also met her future husband Josh, who had served in the Marines and was working at a railroad job. Her independent nature was a good match for her husband whose career early on meant working away from home during the week and coming home on the weekends. "We did that for several years while Kimber was little and switched gears before Barrett and Heckler were born."

Gardening was always a vital component of building a life in the small town they have called home since 2007. "I remember when Barrett was born in May, we had a longer stay in the hospital with him. But the day he came home, I planted the garden that year. Around Mother's Day is always a good time to plant a garden."

Mothering, gardening, and never shying away from work has defined Struble's life. Her career path led her to teach Ag Education in Waverly, Neb. However, the commute was simply too much and there were no teaching jobs closer to home, so she headed to work for a global seed company as a seed tech and then took an administrative position. Then came an opportunity to teach in Friend for a year when Barrett was a baby. Once Heckler came along, three children in daycare and working full-time simply wasn't going to work anymore. Later, when the children were in pre-school, she went back to work part-time.

During her part-time work, Struble started teaching at the Nebraska Correctional Center for Women. "I worked with a non-profit called Rise. Their curriculum is both personal and professional development for people in prison. It is designed to do the inside work first, on relationships and communication. Then we worked on skills such as cover letters, resumes, and how to interview. The second half of the course is developing entrepreneurial businesses they could actually launch after they got out. We ran all the numbers and figured out the marketing, everything they would need to start a business at the base level. I also worked with the incarcerated individuals that had gone through the program and helped train them to be peer facilitators. I have always loved classroom management and enjoyed passing that information on to them."

Struble worked with Rise for three years and enjoyed every minute, but decided to take a position at St. Paul Lutheran School in Utica. It works out well because her children attend the school, and the hours are conducive for balancing work and home life. At the school, she is enjoying making improvements to the library and dreams of one day starting a school gardening program.

Struble is doing all of this and of course tending to her "urban farm." "Living in town, you're really only restricted by the town codes. But we are able to do so much with what we have. It's all about the capacity that your land has to produce and trying to reach that capacity."

Everywhere one turns in the summertime, the landscape thrives and Struble's face lights up as she lists some of the plants that surround her home – everything from chives to oregano, sage, rhubarb, garlic, lemon balm, lavender, and mint (that has the powerful dual purpose of attracting bees and keeping mosquitos away). "I like the perennials because I don't want to dig my landscape up every year."

Her list of plants continues to an entire bed of annual herbs too – Spicy Orange Thyme, tarragon, dill, basil, parsley, cilantro, rosemary, and even stevia (to name a few). There's also the vegetable garden that includes many types of tomatoes, cucumbers, asparagus, kale, lettuce, radishes, onions, beets, carrots, lima beans, cow peas, asparagus beans, green beans, sugar snap peas, cauliflower, cabbage, broccoli, "And marigolds and zinnias around the garden for a good border. I grow most of my vining plants and potatoes too at Josh's folks who live outside of Utica because those take a lot more room."

There's also hardy kiwi to grow, a strawberry patch, blueberries, raspberries, and Goji berries too. "All the variety has really helped the kids to eat very well and try a lot of different foods."

The Struble children all help in the garden too, and she smiles thinking back to her own formative years. "There was nothing better than running around my grandma's house, spending two days picking green beans while they canned inside, and going barefoot all summer long."

Canning and processing their own meat are also part of the family's chores. The couple has built a complete "summer kitchen" with all the fixings to get the job done. Josh is in charge of making all the compost and canning the pickles. They buy bulk fruit like peaches and pears to can, too. You also may find Struble offering beef broth or homemade baked goods to friends and neighbors. And, this summer, even more flowers will be grown and potentially sold as fresh bouquets.

"Everywhere I look there are ideas and opportunities," Struble admitted. "I really am a farmer at heart."

She really is, and she believes the world could use a lot more lawns turned urban farms like they strive to do. "I don't want the things my parents and grandparents knew how to do to get lost. All of this is something really quite simple and so very rewarding. It's really about the stewardship of the land for me and caring for what we've been given. I want my kids to know where their food comes from and the effort it takes to get a meal on the table."

A labor of love indeed she said, "It's about what we can give back to the land instead of taking away."

Circle of Friends for Soil Health

Kerry Hoffschneider | March 13, 2023

Mike McDonald, David Brhel, Todd Kudlacek, Brian Brhel and Scott Gonnerman.

DENTON, Neb. – There's a homemade frame with quotes hanging in the entryway next to the door of Brian Brhel's farmhouse near

Denton, Neb. Inside the frame are photos of grazing cattle and golden fields of crops. Surrounding the photos are quotes, among them is this one by Wendell Berry, "We have neglected the truth that a good farmer is a craftsman of the highest order, a kind of artist."

Another quote by Will Rogers states, "The farmer has to be an optimist, or he would not still be a farmer."

One of the most pervasive questions facing the culture of agriculture is how, in fact, do farmers and ranchers keep their optimism in the ever-changing and challenging world of their industry? Beyond the doorway of Brhel's home, you will see a group of farmers sitting around his kitchen table who have found an answer to that question. They are a circle of trusted friends who find hope and optimism from learning from one another. From different areas and backgrounds, these farmers share a common purpose – improving the soil, water, and all natural resources on their farms and ranches for generations to come.

While attending no-till conferences, the group members began befriending one another and decided to start meeting on a regular basis. Brhel is a dryland farmer who raises a host of crops, including cover crop seed, and intensively grazes cattle. "It was through my friend that I met Scott Gonnerman at a No-Till on the Plains Conference in Salina, Kan."

Gonnerman chimed in, "As we got to know each other better, we decided to form a group where we would meet occasionally and discuss what we were doing and how it was working. We have probably learned more about the things that don't work from each other than the things that do. The group has also helped me try some new ideas that I probably would not have otherwise."

"Having such forward thinking minds in the group gave me support in reducing some of the fertility I apply and helped me move away from tools that don't support soil life," Brhel noted. "Reducing phosphate application through crop rotation and using cover crops are some examples."

On a table near Brhel's kitchen window is a small test plot. He explained the results he is seeing to the group. "Bottom line, the compost extracts applied to seed before planting and in-furrow performed as well as or slightly better than commercial phosphate as far as germination and initial growth. I just had to know if I was wasting my time or if the extracts were performing before I pursued them further and the kitchen was warm enough to germinate the seeds."

"It is about freedom and being able to focus on building life in the system," Brhel said about soil health practices. "Building resilience in my soil releases me from spending so much on inputs."

Gonnerman, who lives near Gresham and farms about 50 percent irrigated and 50 percent dryland land, agrees. "I've been no-till since 2008 and 100 percent non-GMO with no insecticides and fungicides since 2013. I grow corn, soybeans, small grains, cover crops, and alfalfa. I'm rotating alfalfa on all my acres to help control my weed population and build nitrogen."

Todd Kudlacek is also one of the circle of farmer friends and runs a diversified livestock farm southeast of Brainard where they raise corn, beans, wheat, alfalfa, cover crops, cattle, sheep, and a few chickens. He praised the group's benefits as well. "It seems everyone has a roadblock we run into and within our group someone always has a solution or idea to try."

Group member Mike McDonald, has several conservation and soil-enhancing efforts implemented on the farm near Palmyra – everything from pollinators, wildlife habitat, an orchard, and grazing of annuals and perennials to growing corn, soybeans, and cereals such as oats, barley and wheat. "We integrate cover crops to build organic matter and to prevent wind, soil, and water erosion. The cover crops help increase water infiltration and help us steadily reduce synthetic fertilizers and herbicides."

"As a teacher of 32-plus years, this is one of the best learning groups that I have ever participated in and I consider the members good friends," McDonald said adamantly. "I am indebted to them."

"The group has changed how my wife and I view profitability," McDonald went on to explain. "Soil health and water quality demand consistent and annual work. It oftentimes impacts our rotations, input costs, and reduces our yields while balancing with a metric for soil health growth and paying our bills. This year, we are taking it a step further with weather resiliency by converting 20-plus acres to native grasses, forbs, pollinators, and building carbon as well as helping with water infiltration. We also expanded our pond so that we can attract wildlife with water needs."

"The group also helps each other through sharing, buying, and cleaning cover crops. On several occasions, we have worked together to clean rye that peer group members have raised and then we sell it amongst ourselves," McDonald said. "We try and coordinate trips to field days and several times we have hosted farmers from South Africa, Russia, Ukraine, and other parts of the world. This allows us to learn and also serve the greater community."

During the meeting, Brhel passed around a sampling of compost with a small mushroom inside. Group members opened the soil sample, inhaled and marveled at its healthy components. There were also snacks to share later on when the discussion came to an end.

Perhaps the placement of the frame by Brhel's door is also part of the learning and reminding process to never forget the greater pursuits at hand as the circle of friends come and go. Another quote in the frame from Thomas Jefferson says, "Agriculture is our wisest pursuit, because in the end it will contribute most to real wealth, good morals, and happiness."

When it's time to go home, the efforts to be wise in their pursuits continue, as Kudlacek purposefully shared, "My wife and I have five kids and we need to do everything we can in our power to change practices for the better. I want my kids to have the opportunity of a better way to farm, to have clean water, and a sustainable operation free of pesticides and commercial fertilizers. If we have healthy soil, we have healthy crops, livestock, and people."

A Lot of Love and Nip and Tuck

Kerry Hoffschneider | October 27, 2022

CUSHING, Iowa – Vergil and Jacquline Heyer said just one major disagreement defines their marriage that began close to Valentine's Day on February 20, 1954.

"I say I love him more than he loves me, and he says he loves me more than I love him. This is what we argue over," Jacquline said as she smiled at her husband of nearly 70 years who nodded in agreement.

A lot of love is what it took throughout the years and more than their fair share of "nip and tuck too," Jacquline recalled. "Our daughter said one day, 'Mom, we know those two guys pretty good – nip and tuck.' And we did. But here we are."

Here they are indeed – but not without a lot of hard work, worry, and most important – faith. Today, the couple resides on the farm they fought to finally purchase after an unexpected binding lease left them with the choice to move many times across the country to earn the money they would need to gain control of the Heyer farm once again. Vance Heyer, their grandson, wanted his grandparents' story recorded for history's sake. Today, he is carrying forward his family's farming legacy of love for one another and hard work that began with his grandparents.

Jacquline Joann Hayes was born in a house in the country in 1935. "My dad did not have a car. He had a white horse that he rode into Anthon, Iowa to get to the doctor that night. He said he felt like Paul Revere when he got there and announced, 'The baby is coming.'"

Later, Jacquline would meet her future husband in an oat field. "I have eight brothers and they were working for farmers back in the day when you shocked grain together. His mom, who lived four miles away, had poor vision and came to our house mid-morning and asked if my brothers could come and help shock grain. I was helping mom with laundry that day. My mom told her the boys were gone helping someone else, so I went instead."

"Vergil's mom told me I could help her with some ironing in the house before the guys came home for lunch," she went on. "There I was, ironing Vergil's shirt before I even knew him. Then we went out in the fields to work. Vergil was so sweet. I was slower than the guys and if I was not quite finished, he would help me. He asked me for a date, and I said, 'No.' I kept saying 'no' because I was interested in going to college."

"Vergil asked many times after that and the answer was still, 'no,'" she recalled like it was yesterday. "Then came a Saturday night when it was common that everyone came to town to get groceries. This time Vergil came over and said, 'I talked to your mother, and she said I could take you home.'"

The couple both had their sights on college. Vergil wanted to head off to study and become a missionary. Jacquline dreamed of being a journalist. Then Vergil got a note from the U.S. military. "He was drafted during the end of Korea time and headed to Ft. Leonard Wood, Mo. in 1953. He went to basic training, and he couldn't see during target practice so they said he could be in the supply room or a clerk or because food was important to the effort, they could give him medical discharge to farm with his dad."

"There were only four farmers in the county bigger than ours at the time," Vergil recalled. "It was dad, myself, my brother, and a hired man. When I was 13 or 14 years old, my dad was doing other business in town, and I learned to be a boss fairly young. We had cattle, hogs, crops, and alfalfa hay. We ran the very first pen of five in our county of 4-H calves and won with that group."

"I graduated from Correctionville High School in 1953. I was one of 11 children and there wasn't money to go to college," Jacquline began. "But, I got a scholarship for tuition to attend college in Iowa City. I had been working in town for a couple that owned the newspaper. I did ironing and other housework they needed done. They knew a professor and his wife in Iowa City who took students into their home. I could get room and board that way too. So, I did that and babysat their young children when needed and on weekends I did laundry and cleaning."

Once Vergil received a medical discharge, he wanted to get married in June, but his parents said that was too busy a time, so they were married in February. There would be six children in the family – Vergil, Verle, Mae Jean, Vincent, Vern, and Vaughn. Today they have 11 grandchildren and eight great-grandchildren.

The couple was farming with Vergil's parents when they were first married, Jacquline recalled. "We were living in the hired man's house and the curtains weren't the greatest in the kitchen. I saw some curtains in town for $1.98 and we had to ask for the extra $2 from his folks. They said, 'No, you don't need new curtains.' We decided to go on our own and rent a farm ourselves after that."

Their first years of farming on their own, 1955-56, were drought years, Jacquline said. "The first year, the corn should have made 100 bushels and made 13 instead."

"I went out and got extra work all the time," Vergil relayed. "We got by with what we had. I drove truck, built fence, everything imaginable."

"There was so little money and not many crops," Jacquline reiterated. "We had a few hens and milk cows, so we had eggs and milk about every meal – boiled eggs, baked eggs, any kind of eggs. Once in a great while, we had chicken, but that meant you had fewer eggs. Then God sends angels, and they all have names. Our neighbors, the angels with names, were Ralph and Mildred. They had been farming longer and had savings to buy groceries. These angels told us, 'You kids come over for a meal any time you want. Just come, we'll always have plenty.' About once a week we did. We didn't want to wear out our welcome. We so enjoyed those meals, meat, potatoes and two different vegetables."

In 1957, it started to rain again, she said. "Vance's dad, Vergil, spent the first two years of his life eating all those eggs. Later on, needless to say, he didn't care for eggs much."

"I still love eggs, though," Vergil chimed in.

The Heyer clan continued to grow, and the farm continued too, then, in 1962, Vergil had a farm accident. Jacquline recalled like it was yesterday. "He was sharpening knives on the field chopper and accidentally put his hand in the knives. I was in the garden digging carrots and the two youngest of the four children at the time were in the house for a nap. Vergil, with his hand wrapped up, came to me and said we had to get going right way. I couldn't even get the youngest kids up. On the way to the doctor, he finally told me, 'I cut the ends of my fingers off.'"

"The doctor looked at him and said, 'We'll get out the kit. This time of year, we have a kit ready for this sort of thing,'" Jacquline went on. "I'll never forget. The nurse had soapy water and scrubbed that area all over, down onto the bone. She had both hands over his arm and her knuckles were white as they had to cut off the remainder of bone so they could get them stitched up. We went home that night, and he still went out and chopped a little feed for the milk cows."

Through sickness and health was proven time again as later on, in 1963, their son Vince got a kidney disease and was placed on bed rest from June to October. For four years, he had to take penicillin pills each day. He was also born with 50 percent vision. They reached out to the Iowa Commission for the Blind to get large print books and talking books. Needless to say, the Heyer siblings grew to be compassionate for their brother's condition and would bring him everything he needed.

"When he finally could get up, it was like watching a baby calf running and jumping around," Jacquline remembered. "When he started school, everything went very well. Except the teacher said he would have other students fetch things for him."

He also came home and told his mom one day that he needed her to buy three girl presents. Because of his eyesight, he would have three girls write down things for him that he couldn't see on the black board. He wanted to surprise his three "secretaries" with a gift.

The Heyer family journey took them to work and homes in the Iowa communities of Cushing, Castana, Mapleton, Correctionville, Anthon, Battle Creek, Westfield, and Quimby. They also worked on Paiute Ranch, 120 miles from Winnemucca, Nev.; headed to Othello, Washington and then back to Imlay, Nev. All the while, Vergil's mom was back running the farm. His father had passed away in 1975. Later, his mother was diagnosed with terminal cancer.

"The neighbors asked for a 10-year lease, and she signed it. We had thought we were going to farm there after coming back from Nevada," Jacquline said.

What the Heyers didn't realize is their mother had signed a binding lease, not a standard lease. She explained, "This meant the neighbors could farm the land for the next nine years. They weren't renting the house and the land the house was on, so we could use that, but not farm the ground. If we were to sell the land, even the next owners would have to have the farmers who had mom sign the binding lease farm the farm."

A second opinion from another attorney and a judge left Vergil and Jacquline with no other decision but to abide by the lease and work hard to earn the money that would be needed to pay both a lien on the farm and to pay for the farm eventually. That was in the 1980s Farm Crisis when many other farmers and farm wives were looking for work.

"Vergil began working for a neighbor and I took a job at the nursing home," Jacquline said. "We knew nip and tuck a lot, though, and we were going to get through it. We had some access to some feeder pigs, too, and a big barn and corn crib. We bought the feeder pigs and our son Vaughn in high school helped with those. We could make a bit of money on the pigs that were selling for 48 to 49 cents per pound, and it was costing about 42 cents a pound to raise them."

"There's living from paycheck to paycheck and living from no paycheck to no paycheck," she admitted. "But, we did it. We took jobs and were getting by. But Vergil was in his 50s and he was passed over for many of the jobs because the younger guys in their 30s and 40s were getting them first. Then Vergil stopped for gas one day; the attendant asked him what he was doing. Vergil said, 'Looking for a job.' Then he told Vergil a guy had stopped at the gas station and left a card. He was a construction guy in Iowa buying some equipment and saw all the farm sales signs and asked the gas attendant, 'All these farms are selling out, what are they going to do? Boy, I need helpers.'"

Vergil came home with the business card and Jacquline convinced her husband to give the man a call. "Vergil wasn't crazy about going to Delaware for work, but I told him maybe just the corporate offices are there. He called him and it turns out the job was in Delaware. So, he said no. But he wasn't finding work anywhere else that was very solid. After the man from Delaware called the third time, I reminded Vergil of the story about the priest on the roof in a flood and two motorboats came by and he didn't take a ride in either one. Then the helicopter stopped, and he wouldn't take a ride. Then the priest gets to Heaven and asks God why He didn't save him, and God tells him, 'I sent you two boats and a helicopter.' I told Vergil, maybe this job in Delaware is the helicopter."

It was the spring of the year and Vaughn had a few more weeks of school and the entire family couldn't all head out there yet. The man from Delaware sent Vergil a plane ticket. He tried out the job and soon Jacquline and Vaughn joined him. The family stayed for two-and-a-half years. The construction business downsized, so Vergil got another job in Delaware that took him to the Washington D.C. and Baltimore area doing work on pumping systems. Their dream was always to return to the Midwest, so they headed back to the Maverick Ranch near Johnston, Neb. where they planted a windbreak, fixed windmills and fences and also calved out 352 cows.

"Then we finally were back to the house we live in today," Jacquline said as she prepared a fried hamburger lunch with fresh tomatoes from the garden. "Where we went, we always found work."

Jacquline could always find work at nursing homes, and she also had a short stint at Vlasic pickles and then balanced three jobs selling ads at the radio station, working for home health care, and also the nursing home. Weekdays and weekends were filled with work.

"One week I remember we had $60 dollars for the week, but I noticed we had gotten a letter from the church that we still had $40 on our pledge sheet," she said. "I told Vergil, 'Well, we've got the $60 and we could pay the $40.' A friend of ours had asked us if we tithe. We didn't, but we did try to give as much as we could. This time, we did give the $40. I had just started at the radio station, and I wouldn't get any commissions for 90 days until after I started. After we sent the $40 into church, though, I went into work and the manager said since I was so good at getting arrears money into the station, I was going to make the commission right then. It was $400. My friend was right. We were rewarded that time."

Jacquline didn't shy from any sort of work. She also served as a telemarketer for a company that bought and sold new and used HP computers. "The only job I had not taken was at a mini mart and not too long after I didn't take that job, there was a robbery there."

The years brought many more adventures to the journey. Everything from running a pie bakery to learning to fly an airplane, even being homeless for a time. There was serving as a witness to a murder trial, being knocked out by a horse, and even laid on by a cow. They even found time to travel overseas.

"It's difficult to cover everything that happens in 68-plus years," Jacquline admitted.

"But, we eventually got the farm," Jacquline said with relief and a smile. "Because I worked at nursing homes for over 10 years, I saw houses and farms being taken by the nursing home for payment. We decided to turn the farm over to some of our family. Our sons Verle and Vern had helped along the way and Vaughn was still in school at the time. Vance's dad later bought out their shares and he had paid off the last amount we owed at Federal Land Bank, so we didn't have that over our head any longer."

Vergil and Jacquline are still on the farm, adorned in a John Deere apron, she is ready for any visitors that come their way, too. They still disagree on who loves the other the most and Jacquline said they both agree, "The main thing is we are so proud of all our children and their accomplishments. They are all kind, caring people. They would help anybody else, any time. That makes us most proud."

"So yes, we lived a lot of places," Jacquline said looking about the farm kitchen. "But now, we're home."

The Lutheran Institute of Regenerative Agriculture

KERRY HOFFSCHNEIDER | OCTOBER 17, 2022

PASTOR CHRISTOPHER MARONDE AND HIS WIFE BETHANY HAVE A VISION FOR THEIR FARM OUTSIDE SHENANDOAH, IOWA.

SHENANDOAH, Iowa – A dream begins with a prayer, a plan, and a story. This is a story about Pastor Maronde and his wife Bethany (Stoops) Maronde. It's a story that has built its foundation on the conditioning both received growing up on Midwest family farms and is blossoming into the vision that is becoming the Lutheran Institute of Regenerative Agriculture nestled within the rolling hills of farmland and pastures outside Shenandoah, Iowa.

Thanks to the open arms of Bethany's parents, a long journey led the Maronde family and their three daughters back to rural Iowa to serve two Missouri Synod Lutheran churches and to serve God through careful stewardship of the soil. But even more so, they have a dream to bring people back to the land.

"A lot of people are feeling very isolated and alone and are longing to get together," Bethany said, taking a deep, soulful breath. "It's built into us as people to do real things with other people, with our family and friends. There's a lot of joy built into this effort."

A farm cannot be managed all alone, she went on to say. "This land and this place, someone worked so hard to keep it going. It needs to be cared for and revived. It's crying out, 'Someone take care of me.'"

"The Lutheran Institute of Regenerative Agriculture, at its core, is intent upon teaching people how to grow their own food," Christopher began. "It's about becoming anti-fragile Christians, congregations, and pastors. My answer to being anti-fragile is knowing how to grow your own food and how to care for the soil. It's about being able to take care of yourself, so the world doesn't have a place to put a lever underneath you and dislodge you. If you can raise your own food, you have put yourself in a better position to resist the world's pressures that might be put on Christians. It's just good for people."

"We're trying to restore what has been lost like the experiences I grew up with such as picking a chicken egg out of a nest and touching the soil. We're knitting that back together," Bethany pointed out.

"My vision is to wake up in the morning, run out and do our chores, go into the classroom and read the Bible, great literature, and go out and work and talk about what we are learning," Christopher said passionately. "It's about enjoying God's earth, fellowship together, and having great conversations about history, literature, and theology all together. I hope and pray we're able to model a way for the students who come here to provide for their own families."

It's about the fellowship and relationships with the land they both remember from growing up, Bethany explained. "The land we are working on for the institute is not the original Stoops family farm, but my dad did take care of it for a distant relative. I remember growing up we had our great aunt next door and had chickens, hogs squealing around eating walnuts, and we raised bucket calves. We butchered hogs and cattle and had a garden. Then all of that started going away and it got easier to just go to the store and get stuff."

Bethany is highly motivated in her research about varying styles of agriculture including permaculture and Hügelkultur. "I had these 'ah-ha' moments and realized over time there is a more abundant and fun way to do this while still paying honor to all the wonderful learnings I had while growing up. It's just tweaking things a bit. It's about learning to do this with more beautiful ease so we can all work together and do so in joy."

"I also grew up on a small Nebraska farm near the town of Benedict," Christopher added. "We had a few hundred acres of farm ground, cattle, and pigs. I also showed bucket calves and hogs at the fair and grandma and grandpa had chickens. I remember every year butchering chickens and gathering in the shed to process a hog or cow. A lot of the things we are trying to get going here are things I am familiar with and things I remember doing when I was young."

"I thought I was always going to be a farmer, but the Lord led me in a different direction, then He laughs and eventually puts it all together," Christopher said smiling. "Dad retired from farming when I was in middle school. That was kind of the time I also was thinking of being a farmer myself. Then the Lord planted another idea in my mind and in eighth grade I was chatting with recruiters from the seminary."

Knowing he was headed to be a pastor, Christopher still helped on the family farm, worked for local farmers, and a seed corn company while going through junior high and high school. Then the two farm kids met while attending Concordia College (now Concordia University) in Seward, Neb.

"The first summer we were dating Bethany went home and helped her dad all summer," Christopher recalled. "I was busy working at the seed company. It was a common background."

The Marondes were married right after college in May of 2006. Their journeys took them many places including Fort Wayne, Ind., where they served a rural church of 900 members and a school with 200 students. There was also a year spent in New York surrounded by dairy farmers for Christopher's vicarage and then back to Fort Wayne.

"We also served two little churches in Denison, Iowa. I really enjoyed that," Christopher said. "After four years there, I took a call to Lincoln, Neb. and was at Good Shepherd for four years and taught Old Testament at Concordia in Seward."

Christopher loves the current step in their journey as he continues to pursue his Ph.D. while the family is close to Bethany's parents. "We could have simply said we're going to help Bethany's mom and dad and serve a couple parishes. We are doing this too, but it's not the end of the story."

"God was saying this is what you need to do," Bethany said. "It's a convergence of a lot of ideas all at the same time. I had a longing to be back home to be close to family and Christopher has a love for teaching, serving others, and farming too."

What God said they needed to do is well underway in mind and heart, with plenty of physical work to do and business planning. The couple recently hosted friends from Texas who put in sweat equity beginning to clear the area where the institute will unfold in design and vision.

An old, solid barn will become dorm rooms and a meeting area. They are also planning to move from their current home down the road to the property where the institute will be based. "We have a beautiful barn we feel should be utilized in some wonderful way and properties that need a lot of care, too much for one farmer to take care of. A very important part of this is focusing on vocations so that we can train everybody. A Lutheran education is for everyone – plumbers, electricians, farmers, teachers, pastors, and more. We thought we could utilize the barn for students to come and live, learn, and grow a deep desire to love and care for the earth."

"We have been so encouraged by the response from folks around the synod for this project," Christopher said with gratitude. "If there are folks who think it's silly, at least they aren't telling us. We've had so many people come out of the woodwork and that has been just wonderful."

"Dear friends from New York reached out to us and said, 'We thought we were the only ones who thought this way,'" Bethany added.

"The way this world has become so separated, I can't wait to have students come out and to have their energy out here," Christopher went on. "I loved that about teaching in the classroom in college and now we can have that here."

"We can teach students how to use these agricultural techniques and show them there is a better way. What I especially want to promote is the absolute fact that these regenerative techniques are scalable. If they're going into urban gardening, they can use them with those efforts. If they want a much larger operation, there is proof they work there, too," Christopher said with confidence. "We want to model different systems and show them different practices that can be done on a small, medium, or large scale."

Driving up to the property of the future Lutheran Institute of Regenerative Agriculture, there are conservation terraces running up and down the farmland hills where Bethany said, "I would love to see that area in silvopasture, with carefully designed terraces so you could have a mix of fruit and nuts and all those nitrogen fixers, along with berries that would increase both human and soil health. In-between, I envision the positive impact of animals grazing. With animals, you are adding such richness and reaping many benefits. As the animals work their way through, they are fertilizing and feeding the soil that is caring for all the trees and plants that feed us. It's a tightly knit cycle working together."

In closing, Christopher said with absolute certainty, "We want to use this as a place for the good of the church and the good of the world."

Would you please be willing to help this family do just that? They would so appreciate your time, treasure, hard work, and prayers. Learn more at www.lutheransinag.org and/or call/text Pastor Christopher Maronde at: 402-802-4279.

Where there's a Will, there's a McCoy

Kerry Hoffschneider | September 20, 2022

Vance, his wife Ronda, and their grandchildren - their pride and joy.

In the 1880s, William McCoy settled in Nebraska. Later on, Vance McCoy's father was named after his grandpa. Today, McCoy's grandson has William as his namesake as well. While the honor of the name William has been passed down through generations on the McCoy family farm near Elsie, Neb., a will to always ask questions and change for the better is living on too.

In 1988, when McCoy was 16, his father passed away, leaving he and his mom Maggie to manage the farm. "I was the only boy and had three sisters. That was how it worked out from the beginning. Everyone just knew I was going to be a farmer. I had planned to leave and come back to the farm, but when dad passed away, that put me on the fast track."

When McCoy was growing up, the family raised mostly corn and operated a cow/calf operation. Today, he and his wife Ronda's two grown sons, Tyler and Tanner, farm as separate managers of their own endeavors. McCoy continues raising corn and soybeans, but has also found a passion for soil health and regenerative agriculture. In addition to the farming business, McCoy also started Triple Creek Cover Crops, named for the three creeks that still cross the family farm. His daughter, Meredith, helps with the cover crop business.

"Tyler and Tanner were born to be farmers too," said their father. "They both earned two-year degrees, though. Tyler in ag business and Tanner went through a diesel tech program. When they first came back, I had expanded quite a bit, so they worked for me at first. Then we found some good ground to rent and since have split off into our own operations."

His sons returning around 2012 was one of the reasons McCoy began to seriously look at changing the farm. "I had bought my farm when I was 30, and when I was 40 had the sons coming back to farm with me already. We had to find a new way to make that work. We had to look at the expenses in a different way as well as our risk. That is when I really fast-forwarded into a new way of doing things."

McCoy wasn't novice at seeking out new ideas, though. He had been inquisitive his entire life. "I was always one to ask questions. When I very first started farming even, it's kind of funny, but the first planter I bought was set up to do ridge till. I didn't know anything about it. But then I learned how. Ridge till at the time was different from what most people were doing those days."

"It's kind of interesting, one of my first experiences with 'regenerative ag' was when I was custom planting for a guy," he went on. "I really noticed everything was different on his farm and I asked him a lot of questions. He was a dryland farmer and had been no-till for a long time.

One day we got three-and-a-half inches of rain, and I asked him, 'When do you think we will be planting again?' He said, 'This afternoon if it dries out enough.' I didn't believe him, but we were planting corn into wheat stubble that afternoon."

Seeing how the basic practice of no-till led to more moisture efficiently soaking into the soil, McCoy was hungry to learn more. "We are mostly growing corn and soybeans still, but I have added a lot of things into the rotation. I grow cover crop seed and one of the most interesting plants I like to grow is hairy vetch. I guess I was blazing my own trail with vetch around here and it can really be a gold mine if you do it right."

"We have integrated the cover crops very well on the irrigated land and on dryland are finding some success and still trying to work on that. The biggest success on dryland is planting multi-species and custom grazing some of my sister's husband's cows," he added. "Our spring grazing mix is based with oats and will have forage peas and usually some kind of brassicas. I especially like turnips, rapeseed, and radishes. The summer mix is a forage sorghum of some type, millets, cow peas (for drought tolerance), Sunn Hemp and safflower. When the cows start eating the safflower, it's time to move them. I like using that plant as an indicator for grazing. Our overwinter mix is always based with rye and usually forage collards because they will survive a little deeper into the winter."

When it comes to corn, McCoy said his son is a seed dealer and he has typically purchased from the companies he promotes. However, he admitted it can be difficult to find conventional, non-treated seed, and that is what led him to Nate Belcher with Hybrid85. "I planted some Hybrid85 after two years of hairy vetch and following three years of legumes. That field of corn looks really good. I also planted Hybrid85 on a more conventional field, too, and that is also looking well. I was talking to Nate Belcher yesterday and told him I gave my daughter the only Hybrid85 seed corn cap he had given me. I told Nate if this corn is as good as it looks now by harvest time, I will need several of those caps in the future."

McCoy said raising popcorn a few years back also really made him think about farming corn differently as well. "It was a successful popcorn crop and caused us to remember we could still farm without Roundup®. That's when we really started thinking we could start trying conventional corn like Hybrid85 on our fields again."

Looking ahead, McCoy said he is always excited about new experiments. "It's kind of like my mid-life crisis is trying so many things on the farm before my time runs out. I had a local blacksmith shop make some roller crimper machines that go on a rolling stalk chopper. So, I will be trying that next year. Three years ago, I just used the rolling stalk chopper and rolled down rye on some dryland corn ground. It went really well. I have had wrecks, too. I tried that on some irrigated corn and rolled the rye just before the corn came up. That time the rye didn't die. Timing is everything, but I am not giving up."

Where there's a will, there's a way is a theme underlying the persistence of the McCoy family. He credits his parents and grandparents for being ever-forward-thinking, something he knows not everyone has in their farm business situation. "Usually what I hear is, 'I want to try new things, but dad won't let me.' I try and say, 'Well surely dad will let you have at least a pivot corner or small plot to experiment on.'"

Just giving things a try is everything, like the 25 acres he is experimenting on in an irrigated field. McCoy enjoys sharing his trials and triumphs on Facebook through videos and photos with posts outlining the real-world scenarios he is testing. "I try and be humble about it. I was lucky because dad was always forward-thinking. That's another thing I tell people, 'You have to respect your dad because he didn't get to where he is at by being stupid. Be patient, there are probably some things you need to learn from him, too.' But, I also remind some of those dads that if *their* fathers had not allowed them to make changes, where would they be today?"

Another major motivation beyond soil health and plant health is community health. "My wife Ronda is a registered nurse and sees so many people who are chronically ill. I think the public is really starting to look at the health side of things when it comes to some ag production practices, too. Ronda and I are always looking at different ways of taking care of ourselves better, as well."

"I had a guy kind of trolling me on the internet," McCoy said in closing. "He kept saying, 'You can't do that.' He did that over and over on my posts about cover crops and new practices until I asked him, 'Why not?' When I asked him that, I never heard from him again. Asking questions and getting answers will get us someplace. Don't preach. Ask questions. It's the best way to learn from somebody."

Follow Triple Creek Cover Crops on Facebook
at www.facebook.com/triplecreek.covercrops
Vance McCoy at: 308-352-6031

A Name Synonymous with Soil: Dr. Ray Ward

Kerry Hoffschneider | June 9, 2022

DR. RAY WARD AND HIS PRIDE AND JOY,
A PHOTO OF HIS WIFE AND GREAT-GRANDCHILDREN.

When Dr. Ray Ward travels to the Nebraska State Capitol, he is not scanning the horizon for the city skyline alone, instead he sees the remnants of the moraine glacier and the diversity of the soils all around. Ward's name is synonymous with soil and is known across the state and worldwide because he has literally touched countless miles of it as the founder of Ward Laboratories with his wife Jolene. After 70 years, his commitment to preserving the soil resource and conducting careful analysis continues for the next generation.

Ward's message for farmers begins simply. "You don't put more diesel in the tank when the tank is full. The same goes for the soil. You shouldn't apply more nutrients than you need."

"This is why it's important to save the soil," Ward said adamantly, motioning to a picture of he and Jolene with six of their seven great-grandchildren. "The really important things farmers need to do are save the soil – slow soil erosion and use water as efficiently as possible."

"Those responsibilities are on each grower," he added. "We can't just put out the rhetoric that we are leaving the land better than we found it. I want to see it! I don't want to see silt in the road ditches. I want the flood water running fairly clear."

Today, Ward continues to head to Ward Labs nearly every day where his grandson, Nick Ward, now serves as president. He is excited about the future of agriculture and the gradual changes he is seeing across the countryside as farmers recognize the vital importance of not only what is growing above the soil, but also the health of the soil beneath the surface.

He is so dedicated to the gradual shift in thinking about soil health across the state and nation, that he created the Ward Laboratories exclusive Soil Health Assessment for farmers and ranchers. Each and every assessment crosses his desk. He said the intent of the assessment is to go far beyond other soil tests – measuring the biological, chemical, and physical properties of the soil resource, while striving to maintain and grow crop productivity.

To understand the depth of Ward's knowledge and analytical ability, one must travel back through his lifetime of experiences. Ward and his wife Jolene founded Ward Laboratories in 1983 after a diverse journey that led them to pursue a lab of their own. A lab where Ward and Jolene literally handled each and every sample.

Prior to college, Ward had grown up on a farm near Western, Neb., a farm that is still in the family and where he has hosted thousands of farmers, ranchers, and others interested in improving their practices. The farm location is a proving grounds, Ward said reflecting, "A soil book from 1932 states the average corn yield in Saline County in 1889 was 48 bushels per acre. The corn variety was Reid's Yellow Dent. When I graduated high school in 1955, my dad had me cultivating corn four times. In 1955, we had been farming Saline County land since the 1870s. We pitched manure out of the barn and put it on the land closest to the barn. The average dryland yield in 1955 in Saline County was nine bushels per acre and in 1956 was eight bushels per acre."

"Dad grew sweet clover and rotated alfalfa, so our yield was better than the county average, but they still weren't high enough to pay all the bills," he went on. "So, we made it up by selling cream and eggs in town. That bought the groceries."

"In 1955, my first course in college was agronomy where I found out nitrogen would make corn grow better," he recalled.

"Dr. Dwayne Beck and I were the only two PhDs under the direction of Paul Carson at South Dakota State University (SDSU)," he began, highlighting his educational achievements that included a Bachelors and Masters in Soil Science from the University of Nebraska – Lincoln in 1959 and 1961, followed by a Plant Science PhD from SDSU in 1972.

Ward initially headed to work for the Soil Conservation Service (SCS), but plans changed abruptly. "I got a job with SCS and then had to take a physical. I found out I was color blind. They said, 'We can't hire you.' That was the best thing the government ever did for me. That was the day before I graduated and so I went to work for a construction company in Geneva paving streets the summer of 1959."

Ready to move forward with his career path, Ward was encouraged by his advisor, R.A. Olson, to head to graduate school where he worked on zinc phosphorous interactions for his thesis. After achieving his Masters in Soils, Ward managed the Soil Testing Lab at SDSU. Then, after he attended the North Central Soil Testing Work Group in Chicago and met PhD WWII veteran soil scientists, he decided he wanted to earn a doctorate himself. From there, Ward was off to Redfield, S.D. where

Duane Acker hired him to start the James Valley Research and Extension Center, a 200-acre irrigated research farm.

The next step was a call from Dr. Matlock at Oklahoma State University (OSU) who asked Ward if he would serve as an Extension Soil Specialist in Oklahoma. He eventually would be asked by the Medford Oklahoma Coop if he wanted to start a soil testing lab for them because they could not get service out of OSU. "I told them I would give them a week turnaround. Then I found out after I left OSU that I wasn't supposed to do that because the protocol was the county agent was to make the recommendations. The county agent would just put them on the desk and leave them. But I was interested in service."

It was this deeply vested interest in service that would continue to drive every move Ward made to serve farmers and ranchers. That drive was about to catch a lot of momentum. Wanting to reach farmers even more directly, Ward worked with OSU to begin a five-week program of soil fertility workshops across Oklahoma. "We taught farmers how to take soil samples and then we analyzed them and made recommendations."

Ward wanted to keep up the pace he was building and had a deep desire to work for a commercial lab. "I was disgusted with labs recommending way too much fertilizer. Then ServiTech called and we moved to Dodge City in 1977. They wanted me to help start a lab there. First, we had to borrow money to build the lab. At the time I was pretty naïve, and I finally figured out I was the collateral for getting the lab started because ServiTech did not have the money to build it."

"We started testing soil September 1. I was told I would get 60,000 samples a year," Ward recalled. "We got a few samples from coops, but not very many. Then I contacted Harold Henry from Farmland Industries, a large coop in Kansas City. Harold introduced me to agronomy fertilizer salesmen from across the state. I told them I would go out and put on meetings. That is when I traveled all over Kansas trying to educate people on soil sampling. That is how I learned to do the sales work. We lost $90,000 the first year, then we got better each year and started making money."

The connections were building and Ward's reputation for honesty and timeliness in his work were gaining attention. That is when Ed Curry of Curry Seed met Ward at Sioux Falls at an irrigation convention where he was speaking. Curry wanted Ward to put a lab in at Elk Point, S.D. "Jolene and I talked about it driving home from the convention. Then Mark Kottmeyer contacted me and asked if I had ever thought of starting my own lab. He put me in touch with Jerry Schmidt of Monarch Industries. I told Jerry I wanted to build a lab in Hastings, and he said he would build a building. That was in February of 1983."

Jolene and Ward moved to Kearney that same year, but while their dreams were growing rapidly, the agricultural economy was failing dramatically. The Farm Crisis hit and stalled the building progress, "Everything changed in 1983. It was a very tough time. Interest rates were so damn high."

Still, the Wards didn't quit. Instead of a new building, they started Ward Laboratories in a three-bay garage in November of 1983. Ward, Jolene, and one employee began the business by testing 2,200 soil samples themselves. They moved to a 3,500 square foot lab in 1984. There, Jolene and Ward had one full time employee and added one half time staff member. "In 1984, we ran 16,000 samples. So, we survived. We would get the data punched into the computer. It was back when we used the track drive paper. We tore the results off, signed every sheet, stuffed them in envelopes and took them to the mail. We tried to achieve a one-day turnaround on everything. It was all about providing service to the people."

"Ron Bielenberg the banker came out to visit us in 1988," Ward continued. "He said he thought we could cash flow $1,000 a month if we built our own building. We started making plans and went to 6,000 square feet and moved out here in January of 1989. This building here where I sit now is the original building. The thing kept growing and in 2000 we built another 9,200 square feet – then we had a total of 15,000 square feet. Now we have a total of 36,000 square feet and about 50 people working full time."

In 2021, holding true to their dedication of serving each and every customer, Ward Labs tested 447,000 soil, feed, plant, water, and manure samples. They have hosted thousands of visitors to the lab throughout the years and the Ward family farm outside Western, Neb. where the story began and continues to this day.

"In 1991 on our farm at Western we had no corn yield. It grew up tall and got drier than heck. We were conventionally tilling. That is when I got convinced to no-till farm," he said. "In 1992, I told my nephew. He said he had to disc it all level before we could start. I thought we were going to save water and we did with no-till. But then I began to notice the land with the residue had far less erosion. It made me realize the cover crops, rotating crops, and no-till was all impacting the soil health."

All of this frontline experience, touching the soil as a farmer himself, and touching thousands upon thousands of samples, was combined with 25 years teaching agronomy at the University of Nebraska – Kearney. Visibly emotional as he told this story, Ward talked about one of his former students he ran into coming out of a meeting at a no-till conference. "'I was in your class,' my former student said. 'I went home and talked to dad about my professor teaching us about no-till farming.' His dad asked him, 'What does your professor know about it?' But this student kept telling his dad what he was learning. Finally, he went home, and his dad told him, 'We're going to start no-tilling.' That showed me if you educate people right, it will catch on."

Seventy years later, the soil health movement is indeed catching on. Ward is testament to that effort and shared this message in closing for the farmers and ranchers today and those to come. "The most important thing we can do is keep the soil for future generations. The neat thing is when I drive down the road there are people doing things differently. They are listening and trying things on their own."

Motioning to the picture of his wife and grandchildren on his computer again, Ward said, "Farmers changing know this is what it's all about."

Learn more at www.wardlab.com.

Umatilla Tribal Members Regenerating Soils and Community

KERRY HOFFSCHNEIDER | AUGUST 5, 2021

KATHERINE MINTHORN
HOLDING ONE OF HER GRANDCHILDREN, MYLES.

Katherine Minthorn, Paula Wallis, and partners Mark French and Andrea Hall, all reside on the Umatilla Indian Reservation near Pendleton, Oregon. They are deeply unified in heart, mind, and spirit when it comes to a genuine desire to improve the health of their land, plants, animals, and people. Their goal is to share their journey to move others to restore and regenerate soils to a resilient state in their Tribal communities and across the world.

"If you own land, you have to do something positive with it," Minthorn said passionately. "If you want the land to be healthy and viable, that means regenerative agriculture – restoring the resilient functions of the soil."

This is the beginning of their unique stories of change through soil resiliency. The group does not think they are the first to recognize change is needed, nor do they want to be the last. They want to be creative, positive, and independent when making decisions about the natural resources in their care. As Hall said, "We are always taught comply, comply, comply. Not anymore."

Recently, Minthorn – a Technical Assistance Specialist (TA) for the Intertribal Agriculture Council (IAC) – led these Native landowners to test their soil by Ward Laboratories based out of Kearney, Neb. The Haney Test is outlined by Ward Lab as follows: "The Haney Test goes beyond other soil tests and tells how biologically active or how 'alive' soil is. It tracks the biological activity of soil over time, identifying health and indicating available nutrients."

"When we recently had our soil tested and the Haney soil test showed my land was sick, it really bothered me," Wallis pointed out. "I have always heard my grandparents, my parents, and our elders talk about and be very clear on the fact that, 'If we do not take good care of the land – Mother Earth – she cannot stay healthy enough to be able to take care of us.' When I heard that my soil was sick, I realized I had not done my part to help Mother Earth remain healthy."

When Wallis moved onto her property in the 1980s, she said, "We had more than 1,000 elk and we had deer that were plentiful. The elk winter grazing areas surround my property, and they used to come down in large numbers and I would sit on my porch with my cup of coffee and listen to them talk to each other, play, eat and be happy. Now we are lucky to see 200 come down and all they have left to feed on are the wheat stalks that bloat them and kill them."

"I have watched too many elk die upon my property and it sickens me to see our animals suffer," Wallis went on. "This hit me hard this year and it made me realize that I have not done my part taking care of the Earth and the soil. I have also not created enough feed or have the proper feed available that the animals need to be healthy and live and grow so that when we have our hunting, they can sustain us."

Hall and French also want to move beyond commodity crop production into food production, such as fresh vegetables, for their community. They are exploring livestock production as a future possibility as well.

"It's a mental health issue too," Hall said about improving soil health. "It makes a difference; the land is mine now and I have a personal passion more ignited now. I want to use my social work background to make a difference here with the land."

Hall said healing the soil is a way, "to heal trauma in the body and a way to heal pain and grief."

"I feel like it's a movement for me," French relayed as well. "I am at the point, once we get a plan going, that I can go to Tribal people and tell them they need to invest in these types of efforts, and this is where the investment needs to go to improve the lives of all Tribal people."

Minthorn simply wants to ensure generational wisdom is not lost. "My maternal grandfather was one of the last Indian farmers on this reservation. We were raised in my grandparents' home. It's not uncommon for there to be two to three generations in one home. The first 12 years of my life we were in a three generational home. I was truly blessed to have my grandparents in the same home with me as I was growing up. That's where I believe the seeds of agriculture were planted in me."

"When I talk to people, I tell them I am trying to make sure my grandchildren are going to survive," Minthorn said soberly. "People side-eye me at times. No, I am not sick with cancer or dying, but I know how fast life goes by. I am 64. My 40s and 50s have gone by in a blink of an eye. I want the next generation to have the potential to take care of themselves and feed themselves. I am trying to pick up where my dad and grandfather left off."

Rolling T's Custom Kitchen

KERRY HOFFSCHNEIDER | JULY 27, 2021

JOHN AND ANGELA TONNIGES

GRESHAM, Neb. – He had his grandmother's ring, and he was heading to a movie with the girl he loved.

"I didn't have a dime to scrub together," John Tonniges said. "But my mom Susan said, 'I have this wedding ring that was your Grandma

Kaiser's. I would like you to have it.'"

After a proposal at the movie theater, Angela never actually said "yes," because there were too many tears of joy. They had been together since high school, and both attended Central Community College. The couple was married on August 18, 2010.

"August 18 is my dad, Rod's, birthday," John said about his father who served as a coop manager in Waco, Neb. and died suddenly, a shock to the family and his community. "We chose the date to honor dad."

The rest is history.

"We like history," Angela said, sitting next to her husband behind the counter at Rolling T's Custom Kitchen – a butcher shop and store that is a dream in the making on main street Gresham, Neb.

The place is brimming with history. Woven into the genetics on the Tonniges side are butchers, slaughterhouse workers, and more. John said, "It is my understanding the Tonniges name in Germany is like the 'Jimmy Dean' name here. They are a big meat company. The interest in the butchering business for our family traveled all the way to my Grandpa Ron Tonniges who worked in a slaughterhouse a long time. It's just something we've been a part of."

Then there's the Fehlhafer side. This is where John's eyes really light up, "My dad's mom was a Fehlhafer. We learned a lot from Grandpa Fehlhafer about recipes, like his summer sausage. I love a strong pepper flavor and I put cracked pepper in one of our favorite recipes instead of ground pepper. It just gives it a little more pizazz. My Uncle Todd thought it needed some garlic, too. I was against it, but he was right."

"The garlic one – that's the one I like," Angela noted.

Angela is the daughter of Greg and Kathy Naber of Naber's Produce. To this day, you can find her working alongside her parents growing and harvesting produce. This means the couple have extra vegetables to sell and also helped fuel the idea they have been working on for some time – a butcher shop of their own. Hence, Rolling T's and an evolving dream to build small town U.S.A.

"How it kind of started is we were spit-balling the idea around," John said. "Angela had extra produce that she could not sell."

"Some of it was just bruised or misshapen a bit," Angela explained. "But it was still good, and we didn't want it to go to waste."

"I had always loved butchering," her husband went on. "And we thought, well, we could start a butcher shop, too. So, we started dreaming."

Then they talked to Dan Otto, who owned a building in Gresham, the village not far from the country where the couple resides with their two boys – Tucker and Brody. Then a series of months passed, and the Tonniges family wasn't sure if they were going to get a chance at the property or not.

"We just went along, doing our thing," John said. To this day, they both work full time jobs, John as a seed tech for a large agricultural company and Angela for her parents. But while continuing to work and raise kids, they didn't give up on their dream.

"One day, Dan came up and said, 'Well, I am ready to sell,'" John recalled.

Then the real work began.

"We talked numbers and the building was rough, but we picked it up cheap and for the first four months all I was doing after I bought it was cleaning it up," he said.

Buildings accumulate a lot of life after years of different stories inside. This was the case for the structure they were revamping, they said. From bar to butcher shop has been a labor of love and one of a few doubts, too.

"The whole process, I was second guessing myself," John admitted. "Angela thought maybe we should have torn it down and started over."

But the decision had been made, so they kept at it.

"It took a year," Angela said, smiling that it happened and is now complete.

"I did not see the kids as much as I wanted to during that time," John said. "I didn't want them around all the black mold. It was rough that first year."

Refurbishing a building is one thing, getting the proper licensing is another. After a lot of paperwork, headaches, and a steep learning curve, they are still moving forward, John reported. "We are grocery store licensed. We can do anything a grocery store can do."

Now they are trying to catch their breath and garner more business. They are also ever-learning. John admitted working with the United States Department of Agriculture (USDA) in the regulatory process has been incredibly difficult. "I did not want to ask for help. I was nervous about asking. But I admire Al Kimminau at Cordova Locker so much and one day I just called him."

"Al said, 'Yep, but I am busy so ask all your questions right now.' I had my list of questions right there and I read it. He said, 'Okay, I don't have time to answer right now. You come up at 2 p.m. and I will answer those,'" John said.

"I was scared to ask a competitor, but Al assured me he is busier than he knows what to do with. Every time I went there Al said, 'Let's talk about it.' He did not pull any punches. He showed me everything he is doing and his whole operation. I even picked a day and he let me work right alongside him," he added with appreciation.

John and Angela are willing to work hard to work through the many peaks and valleys of running a new business. While they have some beef, John would like to focus primarily on butchering and processing hogs and Angela is passionate about getting those vegetables moving out the door.

"I have been telling people if they want us at the store later, just call ahead. If people need a pound of hamburger or sausage and we aren't open, I tell them give me a half hour or 10 minutes and I will be there," John said.

Angela is also an extremely talented welder. She can apply those skills to both the farm and her artwork, everything from boot racks to lawn ornaments.

"We're in a nice spot because Columbus is not too far away as well as York, Utica, Osceola, Stromsburg, Benedict, Surprise, Staplehurst, Shelby, even Lincoln," Angela said about the market potential.

What compels them most is making the business succeed so they can work together as a family. John said, "At my other job, we just don't get that family time. With this, my boys can be here with me, watch me, and ask questions."

"I think helping to bring good food at a fair price to people is reward enough for us," Angela said. "It's also fun to see people from the community come in and being able to talk a little bit."

Instagram at: @rollingtscustomkitchen
Facebook: Rolling T's Custom Kitchen

The Fairest in the Land: Magic Valley Potatoes

KERRY HOFFSCHNEIDER | JULY 1, 2021

SANDY BRAGG HARVESTING POTATOES WITH RENEWED ENERGY IN THE REGENERATIVE MOVEMENT.

Sandy Bragg likes to talk about the "fairest potatoes in the land" in the Magic Valley of Idaho. Today, Sandy and her husband Jeff prepare some of the best homemade American fries, too! This is proven by the sheer joy and excitement these "fairest of potatoes" inspire all around.

"We cannot show up for our grandchildren without colored potatoes for the fryer," Sandy said. "I have friends who can't wait to see me because they are dreaming of our potatoes – people run out the door to greet me and teenagers crawl all over themselves to get them."

The Braggs do not have to brag about the "magic potatoes" grown in Magic Valley, they speak for themselves with their flavor and nutrient density. The whimsical name of their past location in Idaho has not always been a fairytale though. In fact, it has been a fight to retain what is truly hearty and good about potato farming. This couple is not giving up on their own potato knowledge and helping others through their business – SuperFood Consulting.

"I helped found Everything Potatoes, Inc. as a platform to enhance the organic and regenerative potato sector," said Jeff, who has been growing potatoes his entire life. "My passion is to see the best quality crop, including rotational crops, flourish with the right amount of ingredients. This is about soil health to gut health."

"Potatoes are the most widely-consumed vegetable, and they can affect soil and human health the most. The main industry doesn't speak enough to the diversity of potato varieties and their intrinsic compounds that can actually heal," he went on to explain.

"The grocery store is not the place where health begins. It begins in the soil. We have taken advantage of the soil and water for cheap food – but at what cost? It's endangering society because of the food we eat," Jeff added.

"The soil is Mother Earth's skin," Sandy said. "I like to say we are slipping seeds softly under her skin. For 40 years, I have traveled with Jeff all over and seen millions of acres of land and thousands of fields of potatoes."

"The soil has changed so much – and not for the better," Jeff echoed his wife.

"When we got married, the Magic Valley was such a vibrant county – every mile corner had a small industry on it. Everyone really did help each other out. It was just a beautiful thing. There were rows of different crops, 14 to 20 different types, it was important to everyone in the valley to have long rotations. Rotating crops was embedded in Jeff's DNA," Sandy reflected.

Born in 1958, Jeff's father Clyde and Grandpa Clyde placed a shovel in his hands early on. He stayed close to his father in the potato fields until allergies plagued him. As a result, he spent more time with his Grandma Emelia. Walking the ditch banks to pick wild asparagus, young Jeff began learning nature's role is far deeper and more important than the surface business of agriculture.

"Our neighbor was Joe Marshall, who helped build the Panama Canal and was known as the 'Idaho Potato King.' This was pre-pivot irrigation when we furrow irrigated. Along with the potatoes we raised peas, alfalfa, pasture grass, 12 to 14 kinds of bean seeds, corn, and onions. We had 600-head of sheep and four or five pigs that dad would give as Christmas presents to the hired men. There were also 13 to 15 milk cows and a couple horses. I have memories of my grandma and mother, Ellen Corrine, churning butter on our porch. Ellen became the one that rode the potato harvesters with us. I watched my grandma, mom, Sandy and our daughters go through the change in agriculture to the monoculture we have today," Jeff said.

The Braggs watched the slow death of the soils around them, too, Sandy stated. "A metaphor would be how the white man killed the buffalo. I feel like that is what has happened to the Magic Valley. It is like a Dust Bowl of sorts – a quiet and ghostly area with no buildings. In 42 years, I have literally seen the color of the soil change in southern Idaho – it has a gray tone to it. In the 1980s, whenever I put Jeff's clothes in the washing machine and shut the door, I would have enough of a whiff of the chemicals that I would almost fall on the floor – that was when I was carrying my babies. My first baby has Crohn's disease now and the second deals with Celiac disease."

The couple sees an absolute connection between soil health and human health. It's a connection they have been making in a host of experiences their entire lives. Jeff explained, "When we got married, my dad looked over and said, 'You will need a job now that you are married. You have a knack for science. I have a soils lab that I have hired to watch over our potato crops.' So, I did an internship with the lab in 1980 and then I started my professional career working for them in 1981. They sent me to school to get more potato science education and set me up with a consulting agronomist. I took the first potato science class given in the United States on September 29, 1981."

The 1980s were an extension of the "get big or get out" message in agriculture that started the downfall of Idaho neighborhood farms, the couple said. "The forces really came into play in the 1960s and 70s when J.R. Simplot invented frozen French fries and hooked up with McDonald's. Simplot owns most of the phosphorus mines in Southeastern Idaho. Some of the big problems in the potato industry started in Idaho with a product called Sprout Nip® that just got removed from global use because it's a hormone-disrupting chemical. It's why we could hold potatoes for months in storage. That is all slowly beginning to change with more natural compounds coming in."

Still, regardless of some change, understanding soil health is a steep learning curve for all farms faced with the complexities of modern agriculture decisions. When we were young, we were like a sponge and getting indoctrinated with the wrong message. The soil labs were, and many still are, all tied up with the fertility and chemical companies. They take you out to fancy dinners and say to try this or that chemical. You are young and you have children, and you want to make money," Sandy admitted.

The Braggs kept learning, though, and changing. They had a gut instinct and the intellect and heart to know there was a better way. Sandy was the child of a Teamsters family – loggers and fishermen. When she married Jeff, she said it was like culture shock. "There's a lot of difference between a Teamster family and a farm family."

Jeff was up and coming in the potato industry he loved. Then came the mid-life potato crisis. In January of 2000, as they were going on stage to receive a National Stewardship Award for Integrated Pest Management, hundreds of potato farmers in Idaho were going out of business due to NAFTA – the North American Free Trade Agreement. Jeff strove to balance farming with a professional career working with a crop genetics company that was a predecessor of Monsanto. These were some of the developers of the first genetically modified foods on the market. He also worked with Potandon Produce (a marketer of Green Giant onions and potatoes) and others, always trying to stay afloat and progress in the industry.

"Then I met a Japanese farmer that taught sequential planting. We started eating different potatoes and recognized the flavor and texture they had compared to others," Jeff said.

With a passion for rotational crops, and crop diversity overall woven into Jeff's DNA, he began to hearken his roots. He worked on the Plant Variety Protection Act (PVPA) that was instituted by the World Trade Organization (WTO) in the 1960s. He explained the act is a voluntary program that provides patent-like rights to breeders, developers, and others to make sure varieties benefit are able to cover research costs.

Always seeking more diversity in the industry, Jeff said the "powers that be" were always seeking the opposite. "The so-called 'potato cartel' and their cronies were not looking at nutrition as much as if McDonald's could make a French fry out of potatoes – it was about the length of the fry and the uniformity of the cut."

Jeff said there were all these nutrient-dense potatoes on the back burner while the industry moved forward with fewer options for better health. "The U.S. was primarily only about white, flesh potatoes."

"About seven years ago, Jeff invited one of the leaders of Frito-Lay's few growers to go to 'open days' in Holland. This is an event where all the potato breeders convene. Jeff was busy with another company, so I took the gentlemen myself. The Frito guy would not look at any other variety but the white potato. It was about nothing but color, not nutrient density," Sandy recalled.

The Braggs' daughters are in their 30s and 40s now and deal with autoimmune disorders and other health-related issues they believe are partially from the agricultural practices they were around growing up. Jeff was diagnosed with diabetes. But the family, in their learning, has changed their diet and now it's all about regenerative farming and seeking out high-quality organic foods when they can.

"I call the potato industry a broken system," Sandy said. "It's all based on money. Our daughters will call us and send us pictures of potatoes they see in the store that have been fumigated and doused with pesticides and other chemicals." They will say, "Mom, something has to be done. There are no good potatoes anymore in the store."

"Less is more with all of this," she went on to explain. "Trust Mother Nature that she knows what she is doing. Trust in nature's processes. It's about best management practices – not everyone has to be organic, but they should use the best management practices they can over chemicals."

"Regenerative agriculture is what we are doing. I switched dad to no-till. Now we are using microbes in the soil. We are striving for diversity in our cropping systems. We are paying attention to what is best," Jeff said.

"Our Creator shows us diversity all around in nature. When we went the regenerative and organic direction it was scary, now it is the most beautiful thing. We have lived both sides of the coin. The Creator shows us that when you put something man made on a plant or the soil, over time it starts a downhill decline," Sandy added.

With a new, healthier diet and renewed passion for the potato fields they have loved for a lifetime, Sandy said, "I feel sure I will make it to 100. I can work hard all day on the planter or harvester. I can outwork anyone younger. I love accomplishing things now."

Jeff is ready to promote the vast potential of the "fairest potatoes in the land" to anyone across the nation or world who will listen. "We have to get back to the regenerative, rotational agriculture I learned prior to chemical agriculture. This is deeply important to me as it has everything to do with the health of the soil and the health of people."

Connect with the Braggs and their fairest potatoes in the land:
Jeff, superfoodconsulting@icloud.com | 208-521-1851
Sandy, sandybragg@yahoo.com | 208-227-6435

Observational Agriculture

Kerry Hoffschneider | May 25, 2021

Brian Brhel, right, discusses the matters of the day with his father, David.

Brian Brhel pulls into his father, David Brhel's, farm drive near Denton, Neb. David walks up – tall and slender, built like an Eastern Nebraska "Honest Abe." He asks his son what the ag markets are up to and then motions over to the garden he and his wife Eileen are enjoying. The two men marvel at the fruitful, lush greens. The extra bounty is already being shared with neighbors even at this early point in the growing season. Behind the father and son are a herd of 20 cattle.

"I have 20 lawn mowers," Brhel laughed, motioning to the livestock grazing gently behind them.

"My parents have been so supportive of my changes. That has made all the difference in my life," he made sure to relay.

"Regenerative Ag" seems too much of a label for Brhel's free-thinking mindset, but he gets it. "I guess people need labels. You can get placed in these 'boxes' and I know why. It's because people want to associate with some type of direction. What comes to mind for me, though, is we are simply following 'nature's guide' and natural processes. No matter how you want to label that, it's about observation and using your brain."

Observational farming.

"We need to try new things. We need to think on our own. We need to be learning from each other," Brhel said, jumping back into the pickup to head back to his farm location. "And, I mean, what better way to spend your day than listening to cows eat fresh grass? I have 80 heifers happy to see me because I gave them a new strip of rye. There is a lot of enjoyment when you see the cattle are happy. That is a little piece of heaven for me."

In 2005, Brhel started his path to his self-described "observational agriculture" by envisioning a plan to bring cattle back to his cropland through grazing forages. "The farm has evolved from conventional corn, soybean, alfalfa, and occasional wheat rotation to a more flexible and diverse cropping plan that includes corn, milo, soybeans, triticale, hairy vetch, and forage peas. Beef cattle have always been part of the farm, but are now used in ways that bring multiple benefits with less cost."

"When I started, I used forage sorghum and grazing corn as a way to add weight to stocker cattle, grass-finished beef or the cow/calf herd. Getting the cattle out of the yards and onto the land was a big step. Herd health was a huge benefit of that move. The manure spreader was sold shortly after. We haven't spread manure for 15 years. We sold it. That was a good day. I did not enjoy working on a manure spreader. When things move, they break."

Brhel said the fibrous root system of forage sorghum really helped his heavy clay soils when grazing in non-irrigated Eastern Nebraska rolling hills. "The goal was to leave all the plant material on the field."

"If you want to turn a piece of ground around and you are just starting out, put some forage sorghum in and graze it with cows. Don't harvest with a machine," he said adamantly. "Graze with cows and leave everything there. The corn we planted after that forage sorghum was visibly better. You could tell it even just by driving by the field. The plants were healthier. Even more so, they were healthier where the cattle walked back to the cattle tank along the temporary fence I put in. If you want to get biology going, forage sorghum was key for me early on. Now I am growing forage sorghum with hairy vetch as the legume component. You do have to be careful how much forage sorghum you plant because the legume won't get enough sun. For fibrous root systems in the ground, thick forage sorghum did it for me and we are also pumping carbon through those fibrous roots. All of this feeds the soil."

Cattle are an integral part of the equation.

"Cattle are raised on permanent pasture two-thirds of the year and the other one-third they are grazed on planted forages or crop residue," Brhel explained. "Some of the fall planted small grains are grazed in spring just before planting. Using summer harvested crops allows me the opportunity to plant multi-species covers that can add high value forage at a critical time."

"Cattle genetics are based on the experience and ability for the animal to survive and thrive on forage alone. If they would receive grain as a fattening ration later in their life, then there will be no issue with efficiency. I tend to be less concerned with the color or breed, as I am finding the animal that fits my environment with few inputs or attention."

The cow herd receives "zero" vaccinations or pour-ons, Brhel noted, "The calves receive one-round of shots before weaning. The cow works for me, not the other way around. I am only tasked with providing the appropriate forage to meet her needs to perform."

What are your dreams and your big, "why?"

"There is a lot of faith that goes into this," Brhel relayed. "I hope to be able to share my struggles and victories with others who want to take this path in their farming efforts. In that sharing, I also plan to bring value through selling cover crop seed grown on the farm and will custom clean and condition seed for others while also marketing the cattle. These enterprises complement each other and will allow me to make a living from the land."

Making a living means using tools and technology, but not going broke doing so, too. "I am really careful about leveraging debt. I could borrow money for better equipment; but I choose not to. I am using a combine from 1987 and a tractor from 1985. I do utilize GPS, but I don't have late model sets of equipment. I am not against them, but those things don't create soil health! I have a no-till drill and seeds to create soil health! We need to let these plants express themselves and let the roots grow deep. This means changing and expanding the crops we are growing. That is not always comfortable. It can be socially uncomfortable and economically uncomfortable because you may not have experiences with that new crop or the established market yet."

"It's about investing now for the payback later," Brhel said with enthusiasm. "It's already happening with the fertility I am gaining. I am still comfortable in my lifestyle and I can support the health of my soil and my community by reducing some of the inputs we think we need."

It's all about better agriculture for a better world, he pointed out in conclusion. "I am really interested in building community through partnerships and sharing, whether sharing information or renting equipment from a neighbor or paying them to do work for me because I cannot afford the equipment. I spend a lot of time developing relationships. In turn, those relationships create win-win situations."

Brhel was also kind enough to compile a list of encouraging first steps his peers in agriculture can take as they make changes in their endeavors:

1. Viewing the soil as a living organism is a completely new way to farm for most people (strange as that may seem). Maintain an open mind.
2. Seek out a support group of peers you can lean on to learn from. Those peers may not be your neighbors.

3. Be ready and excited to try something on a small scale. I have learned a lot from simply my garden.
4. Think about your "why?" What is your goal? If it is only money, you will fail at this. There are too many benefits to list that may not bring money immediately, but lead to profitability.
5. You can read all you want or attend all the webinars, but learning really happens when you "do it!" Take a smaller field and devote it to going "all in."
6. The question is not if soil health principles work, it is, "how do I make them work on my farm?" My soils are visually different than only a few years ago. The soil tests are confirming this. I have a long way to go, but I now have a direction to keep improving.

North Star Dreams

KERRY HOFFSCHNEIDER | FEBRUARY 5, 2018

JIM AND CAROLYN KNOPIK

THIS ARTICLE WAS ORIGINALLY PUBLISHED
IN THE JANUARY 25, 2018 EDITION
OF THE WESTERN AG REPORTER

*North Star Dreams: Knopiks persevere with
fight, faith and willingness to change*

NORTH STAR, Neb. – There's a photo of Jim and Carolyn Knopik back when they first met hanging in their living room inside the family's farmhouse not far from North Star, Neb. Above the photo of Jim with his arms around his wife are the words Carolyn wrote around the frame, words they have tried to always follow to point them in the right direction: "What dreams are made of."

Surrounding the Knopiks are pictures of their 11 grandchildren – their pride and joy. "I am so proud of our children and grandchildren," Jim said, as his wife nodded in absolute agreement and they began talking about their journey.

"I see a lot of hope in the next generation," Carolyn said, motioning to her grandchildren adding, "We've made mistakes. We've done some things right. We've tried to change. And, there is still so much yet we can all do."

There are many dreams, heartaches, hard work and hope on any farm. For the Knopiks, their dreams were unexpectedly interrupted by a fight that came in the late 1990s against a huge, 500,000-head hog confinement operation that was trying to move into their area of Nance County and other sites across Nebraska. Due to their willingness to come together with neighbors and oppose the encroachment of monopolized agriculture, the couple has learned many lessons along the way that changed their perspective of what is happening to communities, family and the environment. They simply want to share what they have learned and keep learning and encouraging others to never stop dreaming.

"I grew up right here," Jim said, sitting at the kitchen table where he talked awhile about his life's start with parents, Ed and Lea. "Our old house was 100 yards northeast of here. My dad moved in there after running a café in Cedar Rapids. Dad made sure we were fed well. That was the most important thing to him. There were seven kids in our family. I was the oldest. My job was all the hog chores and feeding the cows. We used to bucket the silage out of the silage pit with bushel baskets and carry it to the feed bunks to the cows. . . . Wow, I look back and think those were some of the most valuable, formative times of my life."

Jim has always dreamed of bringing the town of North Star back to life. The couple talked a lot about how things have changed since small towns each had grocery stores, the churches were full and the communities were stronger. They also hearken back to when you could get far more for your money.

"When we got back from our honeymoon, we had $17," Carolyn said. "That $17 filled up our cupboards. It's amazing how far that went."

After graduating from High School in Fullerton in 1966, Jim married Carolyn and continued to farm with his dad. "I worked off-farm jobs and would help him too. Then I had a chance to rent a half-section of ground just north of here when our neighbors retired. The lady who owned that along with her family supported us and watched out for us. When they got ready to sell the land, they offered it to us and made sure we could handle it."

"The neighbors back then, I miss more than anything," Jim said, reflecting. "I miss that communication we had with them every day because we would be farming and there was always time for them to stop for 10 minutes and visit. Then at night, two or three times out of the week, we would go to someone's house and play cards. Four or five families would work together, whoever needed help. That was the peaceful part of the whole thing. All the mothers making dinners for everyone – so it seemed like every noon was a feast, you know."

But there were changes coming. Some Jim and Carolyn could see, others would almost blindside them. "My neighbors and my dad were all farming organically and they really didn't know it. Then we had other neighbors coming in, bragging about big yields. I remember one of the neighbors convincing me that we should apply nitrogen fertilizer to increase our yields, then chemicals. That's when we turned into being more like what they call 'conventional farmers' today. We were not to the exaggerated usage of chemicals that some were. We would apply about half of what others were doing in that regard. We did end up getting bigger and bigger. I was in that mindset that if I had a free minute, I had to be doing something. So, we added quite a bit of land and then my younger brothers came along. We worked together and the equipment got bigger in order to meet all the demands. That went on for about 20 years."

While Jim was farming, Carolyn was being a hardworking mom and helping with the farm, too. The couple had four children – Ron, Tom, Brenda, and Becky. Then, in 1997, things changed fast and the power of neighborhood unity and the strength of family became more important than ever.

"In 1997 is when the hog wars started. Bell Farms out of Colorado wanted to come in and put up buildings and infrastructure to handle 500,000 fat hogs," Jim said.

Things got real when Jim's lending agent who was also a real estate broker out of Fullerton called him and told him to meet him on a country road to visit. "I asked him why he couldn't just come to my place and talk about it? That's when I learned there was someone interested in the land we rented and wanted to acquire it for their hog operation. . . . There just started to be some shady stuff going on."

At first, Jim and Carolyn were open to learning more and asked if they could let other neighbors know so everyone could be open and transparent. At first, the real estate broker told him to bring whomever they wanted to the first meeting. Jim said, "So, I called all the neighbors. Then the real estate broker called and told me they decided to keep it a closed meeting. That put me in an awkward position; but, I called all of them and told them what was going on. . . . Later, Carolyn and I went to the meeting and they locked us in the community room. The real estate broker was at the door and some of the other neighbors were trying to get in. He would just say, 'what's wrong with the door?'"

Carolyn added, "We told him, 'what do you mean what's wrong? People are trying to get in!' It was crazy!"

The next morning after the meeting, the Knopiks had eight families coming together saying, "What are we going to do? What's going on?" Carolyn said. Then they had a meeting of 35 families.

"One lady from Arkansas called and warned us, 'Whatever you do, do everything in your power to keep them out. You have to keep communication open and not fight amongst yourselves,'" Jim remembered.

That's when the non-profit, Mid-Nebraska Pride was born. For the next 10 years, Jim became the group's organizer, pulling talents together and making sure everyone understood their roles and was encouraged in them. Carolyn became the dedicated supporter and allowed their home to become the headquarters for the fight and gathering place for the group's supporters. Jim said the late Ron Schooley was a major spokesman for the group because he was fighting another outfit – Progressive Swine Technologies – who had plans to build a 50,000-head feeding operation by his place at the time.

"It was like something out of a movie, a whirlwind," Carolyn said.

"We had 180 meetings that first year. Then we started doing newsletters because that was our main way of communicating," Carolyn added.

"Our newsletters were the way to keep the whole community together and informed about what was going on. Within two to three weeks, we had a legislative hearing with Senator Bob Kerrey.... Senator Cap Dierks would eventually call a hearing of the State Ag Committee to see what was going on. John Hansen with the Nebraska Farmers Union played a big role... There were so many people who helped. Eventually, about 200 people from around a dozen counties traveled to Lincoln to meet with state senators and others to demand a two-year moratorium on hog confinements," Jim explained.

Jim noted that Bell Farms wanted to put up 15 sites across Nebraska. He said since they only got approval for seven, they pulled out. The fight was over on their local level; however, he said the fight continues today.

After his journey with Mid-Nebraska Pride, Jim looked in the mirror. "I finally realized if I did not approve of what other people were doing, I need to look at myself... I told my boys we are not going to farm this way anymore."

As a result, Jim reduced his farm size, sold some ground and no longer owed anyone. "If you owe money or are in the farm program, they control how you farm. It's like having a ring in your nose and they are leading you where they want you to go. I was there. The sad part is when you're in that system they make you feel 'independent' and that it's your decision. But it's not."

"It took us a few years to transition to organic," Jim noted. During that time we were turning all the decisions over to our son Tom (and wife

Gail) who is now farming organic corn, soybeans, wheat, alfalfa and peas. He's trying all sorts of things. It made me feel good when he admitted that he would not be farming today if we had not changed."

Carolyn said, "All our kids have dreams of their own to pursue and we are proud of all of them."

Jim agreed. The Knopiks' changes on the farm have allowed some of their grandchildren to have an interest in coming back and their daughter is going to end up as their herdsman, Jim said, adding, "Our cattle herd is a working relationship with each one of us owning a percentage of the herd. It gives them an opportunity to get involved and Carolyn and I a way to back out of it. It's a way of retiring."

But the couple isn't really retiring because they keep busy with a fairly recent venture, North Star Solar Bears, a family-owned and operated business that specializes in ground-mount solar frames that are custom-made for farms, ranches, and other residences. Today, the Knopiks run their farm and ranch 100 percent from solar. Currently they are working on their latest product, a sun-tracking system that gains up to an extra 21 percent of solar production, running on the power of the sun alone, no motor. In addition to their other careers, Jim and Carolyn's grown children and their spouses all have a role to play in their solar venture.

Jim said, "Carolyn came up with the name and our daughter Brenda puts all the brochures together and got us legally organized. Brenda's husband, Jeramie VanLeer, is an electrician and helps with that portion. My other daughter Becky is a vet tech and her husband, Nick Cook, is a welder so he helps make the frames. We build the solar frames in the shop and do the assembly with the help of our other son Ron who is a carpenter. Ron's wife is Brenda. So, it is a family affair."

Jim and Carolyn keep dreaming, too. Carolyn dreams of more family moments in the home that has brought so many people together to better agriculture. Jim and Carolyn also hope to help more families get a start in the area producing locally-grown food to sell.

"I would like to help some Hispanic families come out and live off a plot of land and start their own enterprises. I would like a group of four because they would have each other to support one another in addition to our support. Maybe we could get them set up with a solar unit and they could have goats, sheep, and chickens, and raise vegetables," Jim said.

Whether or not all those dreams come true, is up to time and where the course of life leads. No matter what, you can be sure Jim and Carolyn will still be dreaming and trying their best just up the road from North Star. Their goal is to point others in the direction of their dreams, too. Jim said, "We just have so much we could share. We have to support dreams in agriculture with our dollars and our time."

Regenerating for the Next Generation

Kerry Hoffschneider | November 8, 2017
This article originally ran in the Western Ag Reporter in the November 2, 2017 edition
westernagreporter.com.

Barb and Scott Gonnerman

YORK, Neb. – Scott Gonnerman has the kind of salt-of-the-earth common sense that can be a rare find nowadays.

When Gonnerman was a child, he told everyone he wanted to be "a farmer and a semi-driver." He has achieved all of these goals and much more. Today, his farm in York County, Neb. has visitors from all over the world – Australia, Russia, and even Africa. Why? Because he sees change coming. While some of his farming neighbors may drive by in wonder, his national and international visitors know exactly what is going on –

the soil across the earth is depleted and our freshwater resources are running dry. They want to learn how Gonnerman and others are salvaging and rebuilding their farms and ranches in a "regenerative" fashion – a phrase that has been made popular by others in this soil movement that has reached a revival-like status.

But for Scott and his wife Barb, it's simply about doing what's right for the next generation.

"We bought this farm in 2004 from my Grandfather Raymond and Grandmother Evelyn Gonnerman. Next year, this land will have been in our family for 100 years," he said.

Gonnerman grew up on a farm near Benedict, Neb. His father, Smokey, and mom, Donna, were pragmatic, hardworking people. The Gonnerman farm was not unlike the diversified farms of the past. He remembered farrowing sows with his mom and his dad going to town in the fall to purchase a straight-truck of calves to put out on the corn stalks to graze. In the spring, they would sell the cattle. The ones that didn't fit on the truck were butchered and fed the family the next winter.

What separated Gonnerman from some of his other farming peers was his father's openness to learn right alongside him. As the years progressed, the Gonnermans were farming what is now coined as "conventional" like many of their neighbors. This means they were still discing the land and applying synthetic inputs. Their cropping systems were a basic rotation of corn, beans, and sometimes wheat.

"But I was lucky because my dad was willing to learn and we went to meeting after meeting together. So we were learning together. That was key. Barb would come along, too. It's so important to have everyone involved on the same page. In order to be on the same page, you have to attend the meetings together. You have to learn together," Gonnerman stressed over and over.

Learn they did, traveling everywhere from North Dakota to South Carolina and Ohio. Some of their biggest influencers were soil health leaders Gabe Brown, David Brandt, and Ray Archuleta.

However, the real game-changer came when they came across a simple but powerful presentation by Dan Gillespie, a Soil Conservation

Technician and No-Till Specialist with the Natural Resources Conservation Service (NRCS). The presentation consisted of boxes of various soils that had been farmed differently – from full-bore tillage to cover crops and then a final box with native prairie. Above the boxes was a hose with a head shooting down water to create the simulated rainfall effect. At the end, the boxes of soil were tipped over. Farmers were able to see the difference between tilling their fields (which destroys soil structure) and the positive impact of no-till and covering the soil year-round with living plants that creates a strong root structure underneath.

"Gillespie's presentation got us started. At that time, we were still gravity irrigating dad's farm (irrigating the crops with pipe hooked together on the ground with gates that are opened to let water out into the rows on the field)," he began.

Gonnerman said one of the farms where they started what he likes to call "zero disturbance" farming, (meaning not tilling the ground at all), was a hilly farm where the crops on the top of the hill would burn up and the bottom ground crops would flood out. "We needed better water infiltration on that farm. Dad was born in 1931. As a small child, he lived through the 1930s and later farmed in the 1950s during the drought years. Convincing dad who lived through the drought that we weren't going to water the farm or do any tillage was a big leap of faith for dad. But leap we did."

"The first years were tough. We didn't know how to plant 'zero disturbance' and we did not know what to do with the residue left on top. But after that first year, we sold all our tillage equipment – our mulch finisher, our cultivator and hiller. I guess dad wouldn't sell the disc, but it's in the trees now and we stack iron on it. So, we can't use it now anyway. If you don't have the equipment anymore, it forces you to figure it out," he said.

"We were fortunate those first years because we had decent rainfall and good prices. It is easier to change when times are good. But that is usually when people want to change less. Nobody worries about their bank account until it gets low. We were lucky when we changed there was good money in agriculture – when it was $5 corn and decent moisture. So we were raising as much without irrigation as we use to under irrigation," Gonnerman explained.

Today Scott and Barb are growing all specialty crops. Once the combine is done harvesting one crop, another one is immediately being planted. The cover crop "cocktails" they grow are typically 10 to 16-way seed mixes. This coming year they are trying chick peas as a cash crop and growing malt barley for Nebraska breweries. Gonnerman still does some trucking and is growing some triticale seed for Green Cover Seed; it's a seed he uses in one of his cover crop mixes. They also custom graze cattle.

Gonnerman implements a common-sense marketing approach, finding his market and locking it in with a product the buyer wants. "We are selling peas to Gavilon in Hastings. And we have a buyer for our barley out of Omaha. Nebraska breweries can get incentives and charge more for their beer if all their ingredients are grown in the state."

Gonnerman also said they have not used GMO seed or sprayed insecticide or fungicide in the last four years. "This is a tremendous cost savings per acre. We have saved up to $45 per acre in seed corn costs alone."

What about insect pressure? "We work closely with Jonathan Lundgren – an entomologist out of Brookings, S.D. who used to work for NRCS and went on his own. He has been out to the farm many times," he said. The couple were both amazed how Lundgren's advice saved their wheat crop from a green bug invasion. Rather than listening to the aerial sprayer who said to spray their crop with chemicals to kill the bugs, they took Lundgren's advice and waited until a beneficial insect came in and ate the green bugs.

"Lundgren says for every insect pest there are 1,750 beneficial insects," Gonnerman added. "We want all those good insects around. When farmers spray, they are killing them all and the beneficial ones are the last to come back. Before the beneficial insects get a chance to return, fields are often sprayed to kill the pests again."

While they are bringing back the beneficial insects, they are also saving water – dramatically. "To actually irrigate our crops we average an irrigation application of three to four inches of water in a three-year period," Gonnerman said. "We use an ET (evapotranspiration) gauge and watermark sensors to help us be more efficient with our irrigation. I install sensors in my dryland fields to observe how dry the soil can get without losing yield. Using this technology has really boosted our confidence."

He added that other irrigators in his area are applying from eight to 10 inches of water a year. "We get roughly 28 inches of rainfall a year in our area. With that amount of rainfall, there is no reason we need a lot of irrigation. Leaving our residue on top of the soil really helps improve our water efficiency. As the microbes break down our residue (after crop canopy), they put off carbon dioxide which the leaves of the plants capture and that reduces transpiration."

After implementing regenerative practices on one of their more challenging fields with clay soils and a seven percent slope, Gonnerman noted they went from being able to soak in a half inch of rainfall an hour to a water infiltration rate of two inches in seven minutes.

"At first I thought that no-till was the answer to water infiltration but I soon learned that cover crop diversity and allowing plants to grow as long as nature allows is the real key to water infiltration," he said. "I have neighbors that haven't tilled for years and still have big gullies in their fields at the end of the year. But, with our system, we haven't had any runoff for several years, even after two-and-a-half to four-inch rain events."

Overall, the couple is a steward of 400 acres. Gonnerman is also managing 132 acres of the land owned by the City of York. He was connected with this opportunity because leaders with the Upper Big Blue Natural Resources District based out of York are impressed with the changes he has made on his own farm.

"The city would like to see their inputs go down and maintain a decent yield," Gonnerman said. "They are very interested in lowering the amount of fertilizer they use because of combating high nitrates in the city water. We are really focusing on improving the soil around the city wells. This is a five-year commitment. The neat thing is, the NRD received some grants to help fund this. Hopefully, if we can be successful, other municipalities can adopt these practices on some of their city ground."

Gonnerman said it comes down to focusing on cost, net gain, and soil health. "We have never focused strictly on yields. Everyone talks about yield. When I go to the coffee shop, I ask them, 'How much did it cost for you to grow that yield?' A lot of farmers are not willing to share that information. When visiting with my banker, we look at my average yields and what the price is today and how can we lower our inputs so that we are profitable. When visiting with most farmers, they tell me at today's prices they need to raise their yields to break even. I think it is easier to lower inputs than to raise yields. I have an entirely different thought process – we are reducing our inputs to be more profitable and to save our soil and water."

The Gonnermans are also saving costs through equipment savings. "It doesn't take fancy equipment. We have a 1992 combine and a 1997 tractor. Our planter is one we bought for $3,200 in the 1990s and we are still using it. It is not set up for variable rate seeding or fertilizing. We do have a newer sprayer that is set up with auto boom shutoff and we use stream bars to fertilize our small grains. The most important piece of equipment is the grain drill and we don't own it; we rent one from our neighbor because at these grain prices it is more profitable to rent than to purchase."

He went on, "It is amazing how many dollars are spent in the world of agriculture to try and make up for degraded soils. It's not just ag technology – it's the commercial fertilizers, insecticides, fungicides, and microbes they buy in a jug."

For the Gonnermans, it's all about making the farm better for the next generation. "My goal is to get my soils back to where they were when my Great Grandfather bought the farm in 1918. It's so the next generation can make a living farming – so they can be profitable without needing to farm thousands of acres to do it. God created this earth to be self-sustaining. I am trying to get back to that. If for no other reason, farmers need to consider how well their soils are functioning when handed down to the next generation. We will degrade our soils so badly that no amount of inputs will produce a crop anymore. We can change that. But in order to do that, you have to change."

To all the farm kids and kids dreaming to farm.

Born to Farm, Born to Live

By Kerry Hoffschneider,
originally published as
"Seeds" in the York News-Times.

As time marches on through this cool spring into summer, Luke's birthday arrives. It arrives during the tail end of the busy planting season, about a week before his dad was born – born to farm.

Being born on a farm, doesn't mean you're born to farm. I think of the differences between children all over the world. Some of those born to farm aren't even born on a farm, others are – like Ryan. More than one person has shared with me that on Ryan's first day of kindergarten he told the teacher he wanted to, "Get the show on the road. We've got silage to chop." His decision was made, the farm eventually beckoning his heart home to farm full-time by his father's side, a place he remains to this day – born to farm.

We will see what Luke believes he was born to do. I always like asking children what they want to be. Not because I think they should know, but because I really want to know what they are thinking in that instant. So, I throw the question out now and again, just to see. But mostly, I just watch and see what happens, because it happens fast – oh yes it does.

This year Luke is 14, a milestone for the "farm kid" who can now earn their learner's permit, that first adventurous step off the farm, into the vehicle. That first really big, deep breath of worry for moms and dads across the world who speak the timeless line spoken for generations, "We trust you (son or daughter) it's just all those other crazy drivers out there."

I, mom, am self-admittedly one of those crazy drivers. Ryan is typically as steady and sure as his choice to farm. I sped away from another farm, now many years ago, and thought I was going to never look back. I was going to write and head to New York City maybe, anywhere really – but in the back of my mind, something tugged me back home – yes, I had a lot of thoughts about the farm. I had problems I wanted to solve. But I knew I had to get out of there to find myself if I was ever going to really find peace on a farm again.

In the upstairs bedroom of the farmhouse, drawing, studying, chatting with friends, or animating online, there is Luke, already at least a head taller than I am, (with a far better head on his shoulders than mine). He joins many other young men and women in their own rooms in the country and cities across the nation, thinking deeply about their purpose within this generation. What does it mean to live on a farm in 2021? It means a privilege and a ton of responsibility to the future. That's what it means. It also may mean you are not born to farm – the same way.

Do we have farms or do farms have us? I ask that question a lot to myself. I think the answer is as different as the prints on our fingers. I think farms have people and I think people have farms, too. I think the miracle is when we can stand peacefully in the middle and balance both – enough to enjoy and a bit more to share seems enough for me. But that's just me.

Ultimately the land has the final say. I like that it's all tied up there for us all – where we begin and end you know – from dust to dust and there we go. We sure forget sometimes, don't we? I do. I forget my boy is becoming a man some days – born on a farm, the son of Ryan who was born to farm. There's a blessing in the contrast between the two of them – Luke and Ryan. One hand needs the other. The God of love made it that way. Where the intellect believes they have all the answers, dutiful hands remind him of the work needed behind the ideas. Where the hands are overly devoted to tasks, the mind and heart reminds dad to dream too.

Happy 14th year, Mr. Luke. What you were born to do will unfold by God's grace. I am just so thankful you were born. Born to farm or not, you were born for a big reason – to live!

Want to learn more about the Graze Master Group?
Contact co-founders:
Del Ficke at (402) 499-0329
Kerry Hoffschneider at (402) 363-8963
www.grazemastergroup.com

www.ingramcontent.com/pod-product-compliance
Lightning Source LLC
Chambersburg PA
CBHW052250220526
45471CB00001B/272